KABBALAH: THE POWER TO CHANGE EVERYTHING

Kabbalah Publishing is a registered DBA of Kabbalah Centre International, Inc.

For further information:

The Kabbalah Centre
155 E. 48th St., New York, NY 10017
1062 S. Robertson Blvd., Los Angeles, CA 90035

1.800.Kabbalah  www.kabbalah.com

First Edition October 2009
Second Printing December 2009
Printed in Canada
ISBN13: 978-1-57189-633-9

Design: HL Design (Hyun Min Lee)  www.hldesignco.com

**Mixed Sources**
Product group from well-managed forests, controlled sources and recycled wood or fiber
www.fsc.org  Cert no. SW-COC-000952
© 1996 Forest Stewardship Council
FSC

100%

# KABBALAH

# THE
# POWER
## TO
# CHANGE
# EVERYTHING

**KABBALAH**
PUBLISHING

## YEHUDA BERG

# TABLE OF CONTENTS

# PREFACE

When I was growing up, my parents taught Kabbalah from the basement of our house. I didn't understand much about what they were doing back then. All I knew was that there were always lots of people in our home—from drug addicts to the homeless—who my parents were teaching and helping.

By the time I was 12, I had started asking questions, so my father, the Rav, introduced me to his wisdom, the wisdom that his teacher's teacher had made accessible by translating into a modern language, and that his own teacher made available to the working class, and that the Rav and Karen (my mother) gave freely to whoever wanted to learn. My father gave this wisdom to me.

Yet at no time did he tell me what to do with it, or tell me that his wisdom was my path. I was always given the free will to be a doctor, or an architect, or whatever I wanted to become. But at 17 I knew, somehow, that was my path too. I needed to be part of giving this wisdom to others.

My father gave me my first project to work on for The Kabbalah Centre, and since then there have been many more. With every project and every step along the way I believed I needed the Rav or his wisdom as my crutch. It did not matter how many years passed, how many students I was teaching, or how many bestsellers I had written; I was still this 17 year old boy hiding behind the Rav, needing his direction and approval.

I believed I was unworthy to be a teacher in this historic lineage of giants. I needed the Rav. I needed the Rav's teacher, and *his* teacher's teacher.

On September 2, 2004, my father had a stroke, and we essentially stopped studying together. As I could no longer look to the Rav, I tried to put things off on the kabbalists: "according to the kabbalists" this, or "according to the kabblalists" that. All the while I was avoiding taking responsibility for being a teacher myself. Until now.

Interestingly, in the first page of my first book I quoted Kabbalist Solomon Gabirol regarding acquiring wisdom. He said *"In seeking wisdom the first stage is silence, the second stage is listening, the third stage is remembrance, the fourth stage is practicing, the fifth stage is teaching."*

If you are truly seeking wisdom you must teach.

This insight was the first step of my own journey. *Kabbalah: The Power to Change Everything* is the next step. In writing it I have learned that to truly teach you need to accept responsibility for the whole package, no matter what. To change the world each of us needs to be a teacher, to stand on our own two feet on a soapbox in Hyde Park Speakers' Corner, with no mind for who listens or what he or she will think. To just risk it.

This book is my soapbox, and here I stand fearful and hopeful that you will chose to learn, and one day, to teach.

With love and trepidation,
Yehuda Berg

# APOCALYPSE NOW

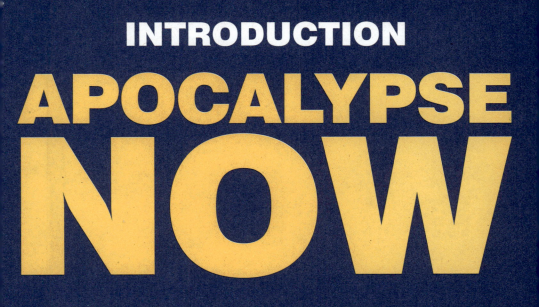

Whether we realize it or not, we are at war right now. We are in a fight to the finish to stop the relentless destruction of every aspect of life. A war of consciousness. The Bible tells us that there will come a time at the end of days when, "You shall eat the flesh of your sons, and the flesh of your daughters shall you eat." *Leviticus 26:29*

This world is meant to be blissful, beautiful, happy, healthy, clean, eternal, sustainable—in short, perfect. And so are we. So what happened? Although it may have been intended to be perfect, the world was not created this way. It was created so that through our own efforts we can achieve perfection for ourselves and the planet. So what is the story with this painful history of humanity?

It's the story of Consciousness.

Our consciousness.

Consciousness is the *essence* of everything. It is what makes us do what we do and think the way we think. It is a hard-wired driver that essentially makes us who we are.

In 2009, scientist Dr. Robert Lanza wrote a book called *Biocentrism: How Life and Consciousness Are the Keys to Understanding the True Nature of the Universe.* Dr. Lanza states in his book: "There is no separate physical universe outside of life and consciousness. Nothing is real that is not perceived. There was never a time when an external, dumb, physical universe existed, or that life sprang randomly from it at a later date. Space and time exist only as constructs of the mind."

Quantum physics basically says human consciousness plays a vital role in reality. In other words, your kitchen table does not exist until your consciousness observes it. According to the latest experiments in physics, there is no independent universe out there. The entire cosmos is an illusion, conjured by the mind. Nothing really exists *outside* your mind. The universe you think you see only exists *within* the realm of human consciousness. It's a construct of mind.

According to Dr. Lanza, consciousness creates the universe we perceive instead of the other way around! Namely, the universe did not come into existence and then create galaxies, Earth, life, and then consciousness. Rather, consciousness birthed the universe itself, including all of its laws. Put another way, there is no such thing as mind over matter. Mind *is* matter. Not only did consciousness create *everything*, but consciousness is *everything*.

Is science saying (and am I suggesting) that we ourselves created the suffering that exists in this world?

The answer is yes.

Written more than 2000 years ago, the *Zohar* explains that the Holy Temple in Jerusalem was not built with axes and hammers. Yes, these tools erected the physical structure, but its real creation came from the consciousness of the people who envisioned it. In fact, all the wonders of the world—the Pyramids, Angel Falls, the Hanging Gardens of Babylon, etc.—were created by consciousness. This past August, I visited Victoria Falls on the Zambezi River, and there is no question in my mind after viewing this wonder of the world that it was created by anything other than consciousness.

But by the same token, it is also consciousness that destroys. I know *The Power to Change Everything* sounds like a lofty goal when:

- The World Health Organization estimates that 2.4 million people die each year from health issues directly attributable to air pollution. It has been determined by satellite that almost 10 billion pounds of air pollution is spreading out over the Pacific Ocean and reaching North America from East Asia and other regions.

- There are 5 million deaths every year; violence and injuries account for 9 percent of global mortality, which is as many deaths as from HIV, malaria and tuberculosis combined. Six of the 15 leading causes of death for people ages 15 to 29 years are violence-related: suicides, homicides, drownings, burns, war injuries, and poisonings.

- A man in Bakersfield, California, got high on Phencyclidine (PCP) and bit the eyeball out of his 4-year-old son's face and ate it. When the boy's missing eye could not be located, reports said, and the young child told a detective, "My daddy ate my eye." After the gruesome torture of his child, the wheelchair-bound father then attempted to hack his own legs off with an axe.

Still, the truth remains. **Everything** is built and destroyed by consciousness.

So as much as things seem fixed and unchangeable, we can change everything.

## WHAT IS CONSCIOUSNESS?

There is an infinite force of Consciousness. It is the Cause of all causes. And it includes within it infinite happiness. Religion calls this force God. Some call it Light, or Energy. Whatever you choose to call it, know that it is the Cause and source of everything good.

There is a second force of consciousness that was created by the first force to be the recipient of all that good. This second force of consciousness includes all the souls of humanity.

If this first force of consciousness is the Cause, then logic tells us that this second force of consciousness is the Effect.

Let us follow this logic in order to understand what we really need to do to change.

Plant a seed in the earth and a tree emerges. The seed is the *cause* and the tree bearing fruit is the *effect*. Here is the challenge we face. Once the seed sprouts, the seed itself vanishes: it becomes impossible to detect. Yet this seed is always present, continually giving of its essence to the full-blown tree, even if there is no proof of its existence.

When the Cause of all creation sprouted our universe—which includes the stars, galaxies, planets, oceans, and the fruit we call humanity—it appears God vanished. This is why we so often feel devoid of God in our lives and in our efforts to heal this chaotic world.

Mother Teresa suffered a crisis of faith through many decades of her life, which is evidenced in letters she wrote that were preserved against her wishes. Many of the letters were made public in the book *Mother Teresa: Come Be My Light*. Her emptiness seems to have started when she began tending the poor and the dying in Calcutta. In one letter to a spiritual confidant, the Rev. Michael van der Peet, she wrote. "Jesus has a very special love for you, as for me, the silence and the emptiness is so great, that I look and do not see, listen and do not hear—the tongue moves but does not speak ... I want you to pray for me—that I let Him have free hand."

Such emptiness and darkness is the painful result of not knowing where the Essence of God resides.

**Just as every cause contains the effect, *every effect contains the cause.***

This means that if you look inside the actual fruit on the tree—the final effect—you will find the cause. Remember that once a seed buds, it becomes impossible to detect or find the original seed. Yet who can deny that the seed is always present, continually giving of its essence to the full-blown tree, even if there is no proof or evidence of its existence? If humanity is the effect of Creation, then if we look inside humankind we will find the cause of Creation. When we look inside man we will find God. Our true essence is God, our source of consciousness is God, and God has the power to change everything. The problem is that we have forgotten this, and we continue to forget!

*So how do we activate the Essence of God within us?*

## USING THE RULE OF CONSCIOUSNESS

There is a fixed rule that governs the realm of consciousness. If we don't grasp this immutable, irrevocable rule of consciousness, we will continue to suffer and die. Rav Ashlag says this one law is the key to all wisdom. Here it is:

> ### Like attracts like, and opposites repel.

When I say this I am not referring to the popular law of attraction (our thoughts create our reality). This is only the first half of the law. We all want bliss, but what are we willing to do about generating it, what work are we prepared to put in? This is where humanity has failed until now. We have forgotten that the work resides in the second half of the law: *opposites repel.*

If God is the Cause and we are the Effect, and cause and effect are polar opposites, then we find ourselves in a reality that is the *opposite* of God. A reality of death instead of immortality. Darkness instead of Light. Pain instead of pleasure. Suffering instead of serenity. Panic attacks instead of peace of mind. Lies instead of truth. Mindless matter instead of consciousness. Chaos instead of order. Emptiness instead of fulfillment.

Our job, should we accept it or not, is to shift our consciousness from that of effect, from what is *opposite* to God to what *is* God. It is our job to transform this world that seems imperfect and dark into what it was intended to be, a world that is Light-filled and perfect.

## THE WAY HOME

There is only one way to return to paradise. If God is the Source of all good, if God is unity, if God is powerful, if God sees the big picture, if God is responsible, if God is caring, if God is giving and imparting, then we must become identical to God. Remember, we do have this essence at our core. It has been inside us all along.

When we forget we are God, we become no different than animals. In fact, we become worse.

On my recent trip to Botswana in southern Africa, my guide shared with me an interesting fact about elephants. He said elephants eat between 16 to 18 hours a day. Yet only 12.5 percent of what they eat nourishes their body. The other 87.5 percent gets eliminated. This elephant dung sustains the other animals and wildlife in the African ecosystem. When the rains come the elephant dung fertilizes the land and helps in the creation of food for the next season.

When we are in the consciousness of effect, not only does our energy not perpetuate continuity, our energy manifests destruction. We simply create waste that fertilizes nothing. When God consciousness is removed from this world, the world is bound to self-destruct.

Only humankind has *free will*. No other aspect of Creation can choose between God Consciousness or effect consciousness. We can.

We were given the gift of free will so when a challenge arises we can recognize it as an opportunity to grow; we see it as a wake-up call instead of as an opportunity to fall to victimization. When we want to have a good day, we are given tools to have a great day. Will we be a survivor or a statistic, Creator or destroyer? The choice is ours.

There is a story about a man who leaves the world and arrives at the pearly gates, where an angel gives him a preview of Heaven and Hell. Both scenarios have exactly the same setting: people sitting around a huge pot of stew, each holding a wooden spoon with a very long handle. Confused, the man says to the angel, "This cannot be Heaven and Hell. They look the same." Whereby the angel answers him, "No, you see in Hell, the people are frustrated and starving, trying desperately to feed themselves, but try as they might, they are not able to get food into their own mouths using their cumbersome long-handled spoons. In Heaven, on the other hand, the people are healthy and happy feeding one another."

We are at a junction in the history of humanity where we can choose Heaven or Hell. We have almost reached the lowest possible point. It is our choice now where we will abide. As the Bible tells us, people will either change for the better, or we will begin the end of times.

Many believe that on December 21, 2012—which marks the end of a 5126 year era, according to the Mesoamerican Long Count calendar—this planet and all its inhabitants will experience a positive physical or spiritual transformation, while others believe it is the beginning of an apocalypse.

We cannot wait any longer.

As a Gemini, I am fascinated by factoids. In this book I'm going to refer to many of the problems in the world today and perhaps cast them in a new light. I'll offer some thoughts on everyday spiritual solutions offered by some of the greatest sages in history. This is not however, my primary reason for writing this book.

My purpose is to wake us up to the simple knowledge that things *can* be different if we shift our consciousness. From effect to God. From asleep to awake. From victim to leader. We cannot solve a problem we cannot see. Once we can see it, the only other ingredient required is *desire*. This part has to come from you and me individually. We have to *want* to change the way our world is right now, we have to *want* to make a personal change. In order to change everything, you have to *really, really want* it.

It is my fervent hope that after you read these pages, you will.

# CHAPTER ONE

# THE ROOT OF ALL EVIL

Many people are shocked when I tell them that I didn't vote in the 2008 presidential election and that I am not necessarily a Barack Obama supporter. But I am not a Republican either. I just believe that there is no *single* person who can make the sort of difference that we are looking for. The 2008 presidential election was really about change at all costs. People felt that *anything* would be better than the existing situation. But we need more than the *offer* of hope or a change in a political party. No one person or party or system will ever do it all, or even do enough. Change has to come from each of us individually.

From a spiritual point of view, a leader is only a reflection of the consciousness of the people. Therefore, that leader will only be as strong and powerful as the people he serves. Bad leaders are meant to rouse us to take action. When we see something we don't like in our leadership, it is to show us this is what we need to recognize and transform within ourselves. We shouldn't expect our leaders to be perfect: they're not. We *should* expect leaders to work on themselves and to reflect back to us what we need to personally change.

Even if every country in the world had the very best leader possible, the world would still not be perfect. If the laws of physics had been waived to allow Abraham Lincoln to serve as U.S. President for 200 consecutive years, our country would still face the same problems we face today; we will face them as long as our consciousness stays the same.

My political beliefs are certainly influenced by those of my father and mother. When I was growing up we never followed presidential elections or joined in the rollercoaster ride of how a president or political leader was performing. Politics was something that had become about ego, like a cloud that looks solid, but is actually nothing but vapor. In fact, I struggled with whether or not to include a chapter on politics in this book. However, knowing that for many people politics is seen as the way to achieve change, I felt that it was necessary to address it.

In our family we believed that the real power to make a difference comes from learning to work with spiritual principles and universal laws. When my father was a young man, his first attempt at making a difference was teaching children. Then he tried to make a difference through his business activities, and although he was successful he was unable to effect great change in this manner. Then he tried politics. He began donating money to support the initiatives of politicians with whom his ideals were aligned, and eventually developed relationships with powerful people in Washington, D.C. However, as soon as my father met his spiritual teacher, Rav Brandwein, and began his studies, he realized that his own vehicle for creating the greatest positive change in the world would be the teachings of Kabbalah.

## SPIRITUALITY AND POLITICS

Before the Chinese took over Tibet, Tibet may have been one of the ideal models of a socio-spiritual political system. A self-proclaimed "religious and independent nation," Tibet's government was headed by His Holiness the Dalai Lama, the latest in a long line of both political and spiritual leaders. When China overran Tibet, the Chinese government believed it could simply demand that Tibetans replace pictures of the Dalai Lama with pictures of Mao, and in this way impose a transition from Buddhism to Communism. However ridiculous this sounds, it is representative of the way politics has strayed from its spiritual basis throughout the world. Whether our nation is a monarchy, an oligarchy, a republic, or a democracy, we have displaced the spiritual intent of our founders with an ego-based system.

Many of our forefathers including Benjamin Franklin, George Washington, Thomas Jefferson, and John Hancock were Freemasons. The principles behind the Freemasons can be traced back to the same foundation that underlies the spiritual system of Kabbalah: putting the needs of others before your own. Washington took his second oath of office as President of the United States dressed in full Masonic regalia, and a painting of him in this garb still hangs today in the Library of Congress. Albert Pike, a Confederate military officer, attorney, writer, and one of the greatest Freemasons of all time, once said, "What we have done for ourselves alone dies with us; what we have done for others and the world remains and is immortal."

## PULLING PEOPLE APART

It's hard to reconcile the divisions that our current political system creates. Politics is something that should bring people together, yet it tends to have the opposite effect. In the United States, the presence of only two major political parties heightens this polarizing effect. Many people feel they have to choose a side and that once they do so their commitment must remain steadfast—regardless of the people or policies their party puts forward. Every existing political group today defines its position in terms of left and right, whereas spiritual solutions are most often found in what Buddhists call the Middle Way, or what kabbalists call the Central Column.

From a spiritual perspective, the ideal is to encompass both conservative *and* liberal. The value of a conservative mindset is that it emphasizes responsibility for our own actions and their effects. The benefit of a liberal way of thinking is that it keeps us mindful of treating others the way we would like to be treated, and of the profound sense of satisfaction we derive from taking care of each other. Most politics doesn't work because it emphasizes the differences between these ideals, whereas spirituality incorporates them both.

What's more, even politicians with strong beliefs constantly switch positions; not because their ideals change, but because they become addicted to the power of public opinion. A past U.S. president once said, "During the election, it's all about change and about taking care of people. But once you're in the chair, it's just about staying in the chair."

My lack of interest and participation in politics has not stopped people from trying to label me. I recently sent out an email blast encouraging people to become more aware of the environment. Many people wrote to me assuming that because of my stance on the environment, I must be a Democrat. Why does concern for our air and water only belong to Democrats? Why must we try to define ourselves with one-size-fits-all labels?

Identity and ownership is the domain of ego. Through ego we become attached to an ideology, to a political party, to a person, and to our fragmented and passionate opinions. In short, politics has become inextricably linked to ego. Spirituality, on the other hand, is intent on removing it.

As Rav Ashlag explains, ego is that voice inside us that triggers judgment, control, anger, pride, and even hatred. It is unfortunate that most political systems bring out these qualities in people, instead of extolling the virtues of tolerance, human dignity, and concern for others that ideally our leaders would aspire to uphold.

There are no absolutes. Anytime something moves in that direction, watch out: ego is at play. Only the ego wants things to be black or white, right or wrong—it wants us to claim that we are everything or we are nothing, that we are Donald Trump or nobody at all.

As George Orwell said, "Absolute power corrupts absolutely." As evidenced by the characters in Orwell's novel *Animal Farm*, give a person absolute power and he will inevitably become controlling, forcing others to do whatever he wants. Seen in this light the *Animal Farm* social revolution was doomed from the start, even though it began with the establishment of an optimistic code of tolerance: "No animal must ever tyrannize over his own kind. Weak or strong, clever or simple, we are all brothers."

President Nixon tried to invoke the authority of the Executive Branch to withhold incriminating tapes from people who were seeking them, including the special prosecutor. Certainly all presidents and persons in power are susceptible to this kind of over-reaching, but the truth is that none of us are exempt from me-centered thinking. It is the ego that tricks us into thinking that we are justified in doing whatever it takes to prevail against those we perceive as our enemies.

Much blood is shed in the wars of the world, and many precious resources are squandered in the process. The American Civil War was the deadliest war in American history, producing about 1,030,000 casualties (about 3% of the U.S. population at the time), including some 620,000 soldier deaths. The Civil War is estimated to account for as many American deaths as all other U.S. wars combined. This was a war fought over social, political, economic, and racial issues. People defined themselves by the side they chose to support, and instead of addressing the underlying real roots of the problem, both sides became close-minded to the point where a peaceful resolution was not possible. The ego finds ways to make us go to war—even with ourselves.

Absolutist thinking gives us permission to attack each other as evidenced by the slander, judgment and anger in the 2008 presidential election. As Rudyard Kipling, the British author and poet once noted, "Words are of course the most powerful drug used by mankind." Words can create real damage to individuals and their families. However, we have become oblivious to this fact. The pain and divisiveness created by tossing around insults is considered par for the course in the political arena. It is ego that allows us to be so casual about collateral damage. Whether the words we use boost ourselves or put the other person down they inflict harm, and in both cases their source is ego.

What's worse is that in spite of all the rhetoric to the contrary, we suffer from a lack of any *real* accountability. And in the absence of checks and balances, corruption led by the ego is bound to take over. The result is that people in power start to believe that they can do whatever they want. Thus their focus, which may once have been on service, shifts to accumulating—and keeping—power.

## CREATING IDOLS

We give so much power to the individual who promises change. We want him or her to fix what is wrong in our lives so that we don't have to. This is the same reason we turn celebrities into idols and obsessions. If we are focused on the latest Hollywood break-up or Mrs. Obama's latest outfit, we don't have to think about real issues. It's much easier to build up our ideal image of someone else or create a story around him or her than it is to take responsibility for what is happening in our own lives.

Journalism originally was intended to give a voice to the people in a democracy. Pioneers of the press took great risks in order to dig out information that allowed the public to play an active part in a system of checks and balances. However, instead of cherishing this gift, we've lost the ability to distinguish between entertainment and real news—so much so that real news is going the way of the dodo bird.

I'm not saying that there should be no fanfare around particular events, but that the amount of coverage given to people's lives—and their deaths—shows where our priorities lie. On a day-to-day basis, we hear more about the latest Britney Spears or Lindsay Lohan predicament than we do about genocide in Africa or natural disaster in China. And who is Paris Hilton exactly? What has she ever *done* to merit fame? As far as I can tell, she has successfully played the media game to create a lucrative, high-profile identity.

When Michael Jackson, the "King of Pop," passed away, obsessive fans spent endless hours twittering, blogging, and watching entertainment and mainstream news channels cover the life and death of the young entertainer. Television networks around the world broadcast his funeral service. Facebook recorded a staggering response to their live Michael Jackson memorial stream (which was created in partnership with CNN). Thirty minutes into the memorial itself there were 500,000 updates posted; 300,000 users logged in using Facebook Connect and CNN; and there were approximately 6,000 status updates per minute. These statistics don't even reflect Facebook's additional support for the online memorial coverage from E! Online, MTV, and ABC News. The numbers reported far exceeded those from President Barack Obama's historic inauguration.

We put people we admire on a pedestal, and then, when their behavior no longer suits us, we knock them back down. Our idols are really no different than anyone else. For every person's prominent strengths, he or she has equally outsized flaws. We are all imperfect beings. True leaders are those who know their limitations and work with them. They walk their talk, lead by example, and inspire people to take action for themselves.

## JONAH AND THE WHALE

If you have read the Bible, you are familiar with the story of Jonah. God told Jonah that it was his responsibility to help the 600,000 people who lived in the ego-driven town of Nineveh. However, Jonah didn't think he was up to the task. He didn't feel worthy, so instead of helping, Jonah ran away and hid on a boat going out to sea.

Several days into the voyage, a huge storm threatened to destroy the ship. The crew became convinced that the sea was angry with someone on board. To divine the name of the person who had provoked the sea, they cast a lottery, and Jonah's name was drawn. Hoping to appease the sea's deadly wrath, the crew threw Jonah overboard.

Jonah found himself alone on the open ocean, fighting for his life. In the midst of his despair he was swallowed by a whale, but in the warm belly of the whale, Jonah began to process everything that he had been running away from. He prayed and worked tirelessly to overcome his ego, which was making him feel too inadequate to take on the responsibility God intended for him. Finally, after three days, the whale spit Jonah back out.

Relieved and renewed, Jonah made his way safely back to shore. He then rushed to the town of Nineveh to save the people there. Because he believed that he *could*, Jonah was able to help the people of the town transform, which is what being a leader is all about. True leadership requires bashing the ego.

We are all here to make mistakes; that is an inescapable aspect of our destiny. An authentic leader will show us that there are two roads we can take: admit our mistakes and change, or hide the truth from ourselves and blame others. A real leader not only helps us uncover our imperfections, but also gives us permission to be vulnerable and thereby truly change. When we choose to hide our mistakes, we are operating in the domain of the ego. But when we expose our dark, shameful places, the universe will actually shield us from judgment and negativity. Paradoxically, the degree to which we expose ourselves is the degree to which we are protected. Recently I received an email from a campus minister who shared his challenges with me. His courage and vulnerability touched me, and I would like to share his words with you.

*Good afternoon,*

*Each week I look forward to your message. It provides me with much to think about and reflect upon. Thank you especially for your wisdom this week. There is a war going on within the school where I serve as Campus Minister. The battles have become intense and very personal. For three years I have been the object of unkind words, rumors, attacks, and rejection. It has been an exhausting experience. This year, I have renewed my commitment to let the negative feelings go and just do my job to the best of my ability. And the attacks still keep coming...some expected and some unexpected. I feel the angst of all those who are involved in war.*

*Your words gave me encouragement: to discover my insecurities, "issues," and trigger points so that I do not allow my buttons to be pushed.*

In researching social and political systems I came across another remarkable letter, this one allegedly written by Aristotle to Alexander the Great. I have subsequently learned that there is some controversy regarding the letter's authenticity, but I found this letter so relevant to this conversation that I felt compelled to include it anyway.

*Blessed be He who opens the eyes of the blind and shows sinners the true path. Let Him be praised in an appropriate manner, since I do not know how to praise Him for the great kindness and mercy that He showed to me. I am eternally grateful to Him for getting me away from the foolishness to which I had devoted my life.*

*All my life I delved into philosophy and to explain all natural phenomena in a logical manner. I wrote many books on these subjects. Finally, in the twilight of my life, I had the opportunity to engage in the conversation with a Jewish sage. It did not take me long to recognize his great wisdom, and he led me to understand how great is the Torah that was given on Mount Sinai.*

*He taught me the inner depth of the Torah, providing me with many brilliant insights based on its teachings. I realized how foolish I had been for not realizing how God can manipulate the laws of nature, and that much of what happens in the world is directed by God.*

*Realizing all this, I decided to devote myself to exploring the wisdom of the Torah. It did not take me long to realize that the Torah is based on true foundations, while the axioms of philosophy are truly arbitrary.*

*Therefore, my dear student Alexander, if I had the power to collect all the books I have written, I would burn them. I would be embarrassed for any of them to survive. However, I realize that I do not have this power; my books have already been published and have spread all over the world. I also realize that*

*I will receive Divine punishment for having written such misleading books.*

*Therefore, my son, Alexander, I am writing this letter to tell you that the great majority of my theories regarding natural law are false. While nature does exist, God is the Lord of the universe, and He directs all things as He sees fit. I am telling everyone openly that they should not waste time with my books. They should not look at them or even touch them with their hands. It is sinful to waste time on false theories that I have espoused.*

*I feel that I have saved my soul by admitting my error. I hope that I will be held guilty for the past, since I acted out of ignorance. But now I have revealed to the public that I was mistaken and that my heart aches for the time I have wasted on my foolish theories. Those who waste time on my books therefore will deserve to be punished.*

*The Jewish scholar with whom I spoke showed me the book of proverbs (Mishley) written by King Solomon one of the great geniuses of all times. The scholar showed me that in many places, King Solomon warned against wasting time on philosophical speculation. One such place is where he said, "Say to Wisdom, 'you are my sister, and consider Understanding your relative, that they may keep you from the strange woman, from the loose woman who speaks so smoothly.' (Proverbs 7:4-5)*

*I feel sorry for my eyes for what they have seen and my ears for what they have heard. I feel sorry for my body for wasting its strength on such detrimental studies.*

*I know that you praise me and tell me that I am famous all over the world because of the books I have written. People speak very highly of me. But I wish I were dead because of the misleading books that I have spread all over the world. People who devote themselves to Torah will earn eternal life, while those who devote themselves to my books will earn the grave. But I am prepared to accept upon myself the punishment of them all.*

*I did not write to you earlier because I was afraid that you would be angry with me and perhaps even harm me. But now I have made up my mind to tell you the truth. I know that by the time you receive this letter, I will already be dead and buried, because I realize that my end is near.*

*I salute you with greetings of peace, Alexander of Macedon, great emperor and ruler. Your Teacher Aristotle."*

*Yalkut Me'Am Loez: The Torah Anthology, Exodus III 6, The Ten Commandments.*
*Yitro 3 Page 154*

In researching Aristotle I was expecting to find the spiritual truths behind the origins of politics. Although Aristotle's revelations about the Torah (spirituality) and his own writings (politics) was interesting and on point, strangely enough what hit home for me is the great courage and humility it must have taken to write such words—to understand, accept, and admit to the world that he was wrong. For Aristotle to have overcome the natural attachment of the ego to his own ideas, and then to disavow his life's work, blew my mind.

## NEED AN IDENTITY?

Our sense of ownership and attachment are the work of ego. Only our ego gets attached to ideas, to expectations, to a sense of entitlement, and to what we think of as our identity. We have to realize that everything we have in this life is on loan: our body, our material possessions, the people in our life, our accomplishments, our talents—everything. What you are reading is **not** my content, or my book. None of what we think of as ours truly belongs to us. We are simply custodians, given these gifts and challenges in order to come to know our own perfection. Ego tells us to take ownership of a particular identity that could possess great power or no power at all, but both are illusions. And this illusion is the ultimate source of all the pain in our life.

Many people are familiar with the aviation tycoon Howard Hughes. Hughes' net worth was estimated to be an astounding $43.4 billion. However, he developed an obsessive fear of people and germs, which started to severely affect his life by the mid-1950s. By 1966 he had moved to Las Vegas, Nevada, where he holed himself up in a hotel. When the hotel threatened to evict him, he purchased it, and for the next several years very few people ever saw Hughes, who had become so reclusive that he rarely set foot outside his suite. In 1976 Hughes died aboard an airplane traveling from Acapulco to Houston. He had become such a hermit at the end of his life that the Treasury Department had to use fingerprints to confirm his death.

We are all more than the one-dimensional self our ego projects, but we can get so attached to one identity that we forget how to live without the persona. Who is Michael Jordan if not a basketball player? When his basketball career is over, does he no longer exist? Of course not. He is a father, a husband, and a human being engaged in life. By attaching ourselves to only one aspect of ourselves we limit our potential for true fulfillment as a whole person. If we choose to get attached to one identity and make it the center of our being, we are left with only pain and emptiness when that one aspect of ourselves is taken away. The nature of the ego is to latch on to that which is temporary. If we choose to let that go, then not only do we free ourselves from a major source of pain, but we will also be open to the gift of the next stage of life that is being presented to us by the universe.

By the way, the identity to which we attach ourselves is not always positive; some of us cling to negative identities as well. It's the ego that thinks we *own* our successes and our failures, when actually they are both just opportunities. It's what we do with them that matters.

We like to put others (and ourselves) into limiting categories for purposes of identification, but people's lives don't fit neatly into compartments. There are no limits to what we are capable of doing and becoming, as long as we are focused on something outside of ourselves. The United States presidential election of 2000 was a contest between George W. Bush, the Republican candidate, and Al Gore, the Democratic candidate. As we all know, George W. Bush became president. Al Gore won that election, but George Bush took office because he gamed the system. That election was taken away from Gore, some say stolen, in front of the whole world. Yet since the election, Al Gore has actually gained popularity and stature, not to mention a Nobel Peace Prize. Al Gore may have lost the presidency, but in return he received the gift of finding his real voice, his true purpose, rather than having to maintain the equivocal persona that is required for playing politics. After all is said and done who is more influential today George Bush or Al Gore?

If Al Gore had been locked into his identity as "defeated presidential candidate," what an opportunity he would have missed! My own feeling is that the ego-bashing he took in front of the American people dislodged his grip on that identity, and made room for his selfless commitment to the environment—which led to the creation of *An Inconvenient Truth*, to a Nobel Peace Prize, and to growing international awareness of the perils our planet faces.

We need to get to a place where even if *every* gift on loan to us was suddenly taken away, we would still feel complete. We have to accept and appreciate who we are when our identities are completely stripped away. When we look we will find that there is always some good we can do in the world if we devote ourselves to it.

Ownership also tends to show up in relationship to other people. We think that because we love people—our children, for instance—it means we own them, and that their lives belong to us. But there is a marked difference between *caring for* someone and *owning* them. Taking care of our children is our responsibility, but owning them is an illusion created by ego that will only cause pain and suffering for them—and for us.

Ownership shows up when we help others and then suddenly find ourselves feeling entitled to a piece of their success. A friend of mine is a personal trainer. Recently he told me that his business has been suffering. Upset by this state of affairs, he explained that once he had trained a businessman with a net worth in excess of $100 million. This particular client often praised the personal trainer's services and said that the client's success was partly due to the stress relief and fitness that my friend helped him achieve. Although this client was no longer working with him, my friend somehow felt that their relationship meant he was entitled to participate in his client's ongoing success.

I asked my friend, "When was the last time the two of you worked together?"

"10 years ago," he replied.

"And is he still a millionaire?" I asked

"Yes. Now he's worth $200 million!" he said.

Laughing, I said, "It sounds like he did even better without you! Why do you still think his success has anything to do with you? Let that feeling go, and your business will prosper again."

Seeing how crestfallen my friend looked, I tried to explain what was going on. Ownership can lead us to a sense of entitlement that, if unchecked, can push us towards self-destruction. The fact is that truly great things happen only when we have no attachment to outcomes. Unfortunately, the ego feels entitled to gratification. This is how the ego locks us into a mistaken sense of our self worth—either overblown or undervalued.

Imagine that the importance of your life's work will only be recognized 1,000 years after your death. If this were the case, would you still continue to work at it? Would you still be fulfilled by it? Jesus only had about 12 close followers during his lifetime. Although more than a billion people practice Christianity today, Jesus never saw this success. Sir Isaac Newton actually wrote more about mysticism than he did about science, but his family kept these writings concealed after his death in 1727. It wasn't until several centuries later that these profound spiritual and metaphysical writings were discovered by his descendants. Scholars who have studied the works agree that Newton was a deeply spiritual person, and that his scientific studies may have been less important to him than making sense of the nonphysical world around him.

## THE POINT IS CHANGE

The whole point of all of this—why we are here, why the world is here, and why we have the political system and leaders that we do—is to achieve change. This is the purpose of life. So why then, does change seem so difficult? Because ego gets in the way. Ninety-five percent of the fuel and energy required to launch a rocket is expended in lift-off. The remaining five percent is used for the rest of the mission. The process of change works much the same way. Ninety-five percent of your energy is required just to overcome the ego. This is the hardest part. The ego will try to stop you before you even start. It doesn't want you to change, but once you get past this first obstacle, change begins to create its own momentum. You may not see any results of your decision to change today, but as you go from first gear to second gear and finally to overdrive, change gathers speed.

There is a story about a man who needed $1000 to pay for his daughter's wedding. Overwhelmed by the prospect of raising such a large amount of money in a short amount of time, he went to a sage for help. The sage advised him to visit the town's wealthiest man and ask him for the money. Now this wealthy man was renowned for being exceptionally tight-fisted with his money. Although many people had asked him for loans throughout the years, he had never given money to anyone.

Following the sage's advice, the man went to visit the miser. He asked him for the $1000, but the miser shook his head. However, just as the man was leaving, the miser offered him a penny. Insulted by the size of the offered gift, the supplicant simply turned and walked away. Distraught, he went back to the sage and explained what had happened.

The sage told him to go back and accept the penny. "But that will not bring me anywhere close to what I need to raise for the wedding, which is *this* week!" the man exclaimed.

"Just trust me, and do as I say," the sage replied.

So back the man went, and again the miser offered him the penny. This time the man accepted it. Then, just as the man was turning to leave, the miser offered him a quarter. The man accepted this as well, and started to leave again. The miser then offered him a dollar. Then $20. Then, $100. It was not long before the man had obtained the full $1000 he needed.

Elated, he rushed back to tell the sage the good news, and to ask him a question. "How did you know that the miser would help me? He has never given money to anyone!"

The sage explained that all his life the miser had *wanted* to be generous. However, he didn't know how to give. He was only able to part with a penny, and whenever he offered it, no one would accept. When this man accepted the penny from the miser, the act of giving felt so good that the miser wanted to give more. And the more he gave, the more he wanted to give.

The same is true for the rest of us. Once we open ourselves to change, this first act creates an appetite for even more change. We begin to want more and more growth in our lives, and this desire is supported by a growing certainty that we *can* change.

Rav Brandwein explained that the difference between those who make the transformation and those that do not is that those who change *know* at the outset that they *will* change; those who do not, lack this conviction. We need to know there is a process, and to trust in it. Just because a fruit is not ripe now does not mean it will never be sweet. We have to embrace the journey and not let the ego trap us in its desire for immediate results, or lock us into an inflexible sense of our identity. When an opportunity comes to have your ego bashed, as hard as it is—and trust me it is the hardest thing you will ever have to do—just take it. Put your head down and take it: like a man, like a woman, like Al Gore, or like Aristotle.

Zusha was one of the great sages of all time. He lived around 250 years ago and often went from town to town teaching and helping people with their issues. This, as he saw it, was his mission in life. In one of the towns Zusha traveled to, he stumbled on a big party. Driven by curiosity, he went closer to see what was happening. He observed that the people inside were not dancing or celebrating. They were mostly sitting with their heads bowed, talking softly to each other. Confused, he asked a passerby, "Why is everyone so sad?"

He was told, "Well, there was supposed to be a big wedding tonight. Unfortunately, the family lost all the money they had saved for the wedding and will no longer be able to pay for it."

So Zusha asked, "Do you know how much money was lost?" He was told the precise amount.

Early the next day, Zusha came back to the village, exclaiming, "I have found the missing money!" He then approached the family with a bundle and passed it over to them. Shocked, they began to count it and discovered that miraculously it was the exact amount they had accumulated for the wedding. Just as they began thanking Zusha for this generosity, he stopped them and said, "Wait a moment. Hold your thanks. I'm the one who found the money, and I could have kept it myself, but I did not. Don't you think I deserve a reward?" He insisted that he would not leave the village until he was paid a fee for recovering the money.

The villagers were stunned. They had been prepared to make Zusha a hero, only to find out that he was just as greedy as the next person, if not more so. The townspeople became furious, and some began to suggest that Zusha himself had stolen the money in order to claim the reward. A few hours later Zusha was run out of town for his disgraceful behavior.

Upon returning home he went to his teacher, who had already heard the news. Zusha's teacher asked, "I'm assuming that you didn't find the money. Knowing the kind of person you are, I'm guessing that you actually gave the family your own money. But what was this business of demanding a reward?"

Zusha replied, "You know, just as I was about to give the bride and groom my own money, I said to myself: *Zusha, how many people in the world would do what you're about to do? Nobody.* I started feeling so good about myself that I realized my ego was showing up. So I had to quickly devise a plan to give the wedding couple the money without feeding my ego at the same time. I decided that being run out of town for my greediness would be humiliating enough so that my ego could no longer get in the way."

## OUR MISSION

The mission to find and destroy our own ego will push us to greatness. It is one of the boldest risks we can take. This is what gets us out of our comfort zone so we can really make a difference in this world. When we get past our ego we are able to see real solutions because suddenly we are open to see what we don't know. This gives us the power to ask questions, and to not accept things as they seem. We have to dig deeper in order to find "out of the box" answers that can drive us forward to a brighter future.

How many politicians think that because *they* put a policy or plan in place that they deserve more power and greater accolades? As Al Gore has made evident, it is not our successes that really matter; it is what we do with our *failures* that makes us, and our work, great in this world. Humiliation is actually one of the fastest ways to target the ego. The desire to feel praised and recognized is a telltale sign that the ego is thriving. But if enough people can start to fully see their ego at work and destroy it we will achieve a critical mass, and the world will change.

As the Baal Shem Tov explained, everything that we see in others is truly a reflection of our own ego. When we see something in someone else that especially bothers us, what we are really seeing is our own ego. What's more, the reason we see it when we do is because this is the ideal time to bring the ego down.

During the process of writing this book, I have been working on my own changes and challenges. It was no coincidence that throughout this chapter, I had three major arguments with some of the most important people in my life. I'm grateful to those loved ones, especially my mom, to whom I owe the greatest thank you, for they showed me where my ego lies.

# CHAPTER TWO

# MY NANNY WAS A SUICIDE BOMBER

When I was 6 years old, I had a nanny. Two, actually. And they were both teenage boys.

My father was teaching at the University in Jerusalem. On occasion he and my mother would travel to Tel Aviv and other parts of Israel to teach. While my parents were away, Yasir and Sufian Jabarin looked after my brother and me. They were the teenage sons of an Arab family that was friendly with mine.

It was somewhat unusual for a Jewish family to be so close to an Arab family. However, not long after we moved to Jerusalem, my parents had befriended a number of Arabs. They felt they had an affinity with spiritual Muslims and quickly became part of the Muslim community. Their Muslim friends invited them to spend time in the mountains of Jericho and in the city of Jenine, some of the most volatile areas in the region. My parents would shop in the markets of Bethlehem and Ramala and travel to holy sites.

Of the two sons that watched us, Yasir Jabarin was the older one. He was mischievous by nature—always getting into trouble, or up to something. In fact, on one occasion, Yasir was bold enough to steal a camera from my aunt! My father simply spoke to his father, who had him promptly return the camera. Sufian, the younger brother, was the polar opposite. He was a quiet, sensitive person, someone who could always be counted on. Sufian was fun and generous, and we would spend our time together laughing and watching Arab cartoons that Sufian translated for us. After getting to know him and his brother for more than two years, we felt undeniably close to Yasir and Sufian. They were family.

After we moved back to the United States, my father wanted to travel back to Israel to visit the Shiloach spring, a cold-water spring used since Biblical times as a spiritual bath. But the Intifada, an Islamist-led uprising that had started in the occupied territories, was raging, making a trip to the spring dangerous, to say the least. Once again the Jabarin family showed their generous spirit by using their influence to help get us there safely.

Twelve years later, I was sitting next to my father on a plane. My father was engrossed in a copy of *Time* magazine, when he looked up at me. "What is Rashad doing in this magazine?" He said. Rashad was the father of Yasir and Sufian, and I had no idea why he would appear in *Time*. I looked down at the picture he was referring to. It was a head shot, one of several photographs of suicide bombers displayed across the page. As my father read on, it turned out that the photo wasn't actually Rashad but rather it was the spitting image of him—his adult son, Sufian, the kind, generous, trustworthy young boy who laughed and played with us so many years before.

Not only had Sufian blown himself up, he had done so right in our old neighborhood. Reports indicated that the force of the explosion was so great that it set nearby traffic on fire and blew out the windows on buildings a block away. At least one passenger of the bus in which Sufian had detonated his explosive belt was decapitated, another was found suspended on a shard of metal that was once the roof of the bus, while most others remained in their seats, incinerated by flames. Twenty-four people died.

Disbelief doesn't begin to describe my reaction to the news. How could someone so kind do something so tragic? And more poignantly, how could he have done it in the name of Islam, a religion that at its core is about peace? How does someone so caring and thoughtful become someone capable of taking the lives of others? How could something so right go so wrong?

## RELIGION GONE WRONG

Sufian's act against humanity was a fatal consequence of religion— more specifically, of religion when it morphs from being a divine gift to an insidious poison. Religion gone wrong busies itself with doctrines that proclaim it has the right way to worship and connect to God. Dogma undermines tolerance for others. Guilt takes the place of transformation. The result of this is exemplified in every brutal act played out in God's name. God has many different names, but dogma, intolerance, hatred, and murder are not among them. God's Names actually refer to the different attributes of the Creator, and those attributes are exclusively loving, embracing, and tolerant of all people, of all faiths, from all walks of life. Period.

In 1994, on the day of the festive Jewish holiday of Purim, a man named Baruch Goldstein walked into the Tomb of the Patriarchs in Hebron, a site holy to both Jews and Muslims. He then opened fire on a room full of people in prayer. He murdered 39 people and wounded another 150. Goldstein was beaten to death at the scene and never brought to trial, and it is believed that the massacre was his attempt to act out an interpretation of a portion of the Purim story by proactively killing those he believed might eventually kill Jews. However, Goldstein's poison didn't stop there. In the weeks following the shooting, a string of riots led to the senseless deaths of an additional 25 Palestinians and five Israelis.

All in the name of God.

But how can killing others and inflicting terror be God's will or his work? Religion in its pure form was meant to bring us happiness beyond comprehension—not unimaginable death and destruction.

## A SYSTEM OF TRUTH

Religion was originally intended to be a system with one goal only: To connect us to the Light of God, the source of everything good. However, when we misconstrue its purpose and abuse our fellow human beings, when we twist religion into something that it was never designed to be, we create far more darkness than Light. We create separation instead of unity, death instead of continuity, and hatred instead of love. Religion exercised in the name of the ego instead of the Creator hardens a person's heart. Compassion for others falls by the wayside, paving the way for terrible suffering. The way in which we practice our religion can mean the difference between life and death.

More people have died in the name of God than have died from all diseases, crimes, and natural disasters. Men, women, and even children have taken the lives of others as well as their own to show their commitment to "God," to "their" religion, and to their belief in a divine afterlife.

## HONOR KILLING

In May 2007, a young Kurdish girl living in Iraq was brutally stoned to death by the men in her own family for falling in love with a teenage boy of the "wrong religion." A large crowd gathered to watch as she was dragged out of her home and into the street where a group of eight or nine men hurled stones at her for half an hour, until she died. The members of the Yezidi group, of which her family was a member, called this act an "honor killing."

Killing a young girl for falling in love. Think about the absurdity of this. Romans, Christians, Jews, Muslims, and almost all other organized forms of worship have senselessly killed in an attempt to punish, to keep their followers in line, and to make examples of their fellow human beings. They have taken religion and turned it into a cruel and heartless judge. God has been left out of the equation entirely.

Perhaps one of the maddest bouts of religious fanaticism dates back to the Crusades. The Crusaders of Christian Europe fought mainly against Muslims, but no one was immune to the devastation of those religious wars. The death toll soared into the millions. What could possibly drive the Crusaders to this level of brutality? They would tell you that it was the will of God that drove them into battle, led them to commit genocide, and justified raping an entire continent.

But it wasn't God. How could it be God? A source of goodness, of love beyond our comprehension cannot possibly be the force behind such destruction. Negativity cannot come from positive energy. Darkness cannot come from Light.

God doesn't goad us to madness. Ego does. In fact, some historians now believe that the mass carnage of the Crusades had little to do with God and much to do with obtaining control over key trade routes. Others theorize that the Crusades were really about obtaining the Holy Land of Jerusalem and the spiritual technology rumored to be buried there. Regardless, the bloodshed and brutality of the Crusades make it powerfully clear that the ego-driven motivation of gaining control was far greater than any spiritually motivated connection to the Creator.

I would like to note that a movement existed during this time to bring Christians and Israelites together. Nine knights, otherwise known as the Knights Templar, had originally been charged to protect pilgrims as they made their way to visit the Holy City. But their mission grew larger, and along with it their wealth and power. They uncovered a treasure that they described as a "technology" that could unite people, but their mission was thwarted. They had become a financial, political, and religious threat—a threat that needed to be crushed.

In what many historians have described as a great injustice, Pope Clement and King Philip IV of France worked together to create a list of false charges against the Templars. On Friday, October 13, 1307, the Order of the Knights Templar was officially forced to disband. But the purge didn't stop there. Over 15,000 Templars were arrested, tortured, and murdered. Again, religion—in its mutated form—had reared its ugly head.

## THE GIFT

Religion's real message and gift was becoming increasingly lost in the fog of politics, ego, and greed. Religion was intended to be a system of empowerment, a system that would allow each person to connect to God through whatever path they chose. Jesus, Buddha, Mohammed—these individuals were all pathways to the same destination. You can call it Happiness. You can call it Enlightenment. It occurs when we recognize the love within us, and therefore can reach out to bring peace and love to others. It's a state of consciousness where we see others as an extension of ourselves, where we give the care, love, and concern that we desire to receive. That is what it means to have a spiritual awakening. It can happen to anyone, anywhere. One of my favorite contemporary stories of awakening comes from an Internet blog.

### "The Day The Curtain Came Down"

On Wednesday, February 27, 2008 at 5:30a.m. while working for a sanitation company in New York City, my co-worker (Sampson) and I were at the 59th Street dump dropping our load of garbage we had picked up that night. The whole night I remember praying and meditating, asking God certain questions in my mind as I usually would do while working. While my co-worker was dumping the garbage from our truck into the barge below, I was on the other side of the truck with my eyes closed, half asleep and half still meditating. When I heard that the garbage had stopped dumping I opened my eyes and on the ground still wrapped in plastic was a book. *Huh*, I thought. *I've been needing a new Bible and this looked to be one. Nice one, God!* But when I picked it up there was no writing on the front cover. *Very odd,* I thought. So I put it in the truck and took it with me anyway.

When I arrived home I pulled out the book and saw on the back the word "*Zohar*," with an 11 on the side of the book. After figuring out how to read it because the writing is from right to left, I familiarized myself with some of the words and meanings in the book's glossary and began to read. Once I read the first page a light (metaphorically speaking) went off in my head, and I was truly enlightened by what I discovered. I paused for a moment to think about the wisdom I had just been blessed with. While at that moment I started hearing something that sounded as if it was coming from my roof. All of a sudden, "BOOM!" The curtains in my room fell down. (Literally.)

### "Butterfly Dreams"

The next day I went on the Internet to find out where this book came from, and found a location here in Manhattan. So I went to the location and told the people there my story. They were amazed at what happened to me and pointed me towards some books that would help me begin my journey. The first book I read was *The Power of Kabbalah*. After reading that book, everything started to make sense. This book answered the very questions I was asking God all along. Most of the answers He had already given me, but I assumed it was just my mind producing its own theories. After that I read the book *True Prosperity* and every book in *The Wisdom Box*. After that I decided to put Kabbalah to work in my life. The first week was very difficult but I made it through without a single reactive moment. By that weekend I went to church and sang and praised and even asked one of our members if I could pray with him for the healing of some illnesses he has been going through. These are things I never would have done a week before.

The second week was even harder than the first. There was a point when I wanted to give up and give in to my thoughts of, *This Kabbalah isn't working, let's just go back to the old way of doing things*. And I just could not shake those feelings. Then I remembered one of the Kabbalah tools, which is to take your mind off your problems and help someone else out with theirs. So that night at work I tried very hard to be as helpful to my co-worker as possible. He and I don't get along at all, but that night I treated him like royalty. Helping him with his portion of the load, driving for him when he got tired. I know he thought I must have bumped my head. But since that day, we've had no problems between us. That morning after work I was home sleeping. When I rolled over and saw a butterfly right in front of me, so close it looked as if it would land on my nose. So I rolled over and went back to sleep thinking, *I'll just deal with it later*. When I woke up again, my first reaction was to look for the butterfly. But then I thought, *Wait a minute, it is winter time in the Bronx and all my windows are shut, what am I, crazy? I had to be dreaming*. But after pondering that dream all day, I realized what it meant. That something in me had changed, just like a caterpillar, in time, changes into a butterfly.

### "The Journey"

I am truly excited about the life that is ahead of me. Where there was darkness within me, now there is light. Where there was anxiety, now there is joy. And where there was doubt, now there is certainty. And all the praise belongs to God, "blessed be His name." For he is the giver of all that we possess. But above all things that can be acquired, I will seek wisdom. Wisdom is an ally no man can do without. It was here before us and will be here when life as we know it is gone.

You see, when we acquire wisdom, we are blessed with the main ingredient that played a major role in the creation of our entire existence. And to me, that is worth searching for. But I will not just search in high, lofty places. Or just in churches or synagogues. But I will seek wisdom everywhere and in everything. Even if it means searching through a little garbage.

God Bless the writers of the books, *The Power of Kabbalah*, *True Prosperity*, and so many more. And thank you for your endless efforts to bring Light into the World.

Religion at its root is designed to engender this profound change of heart. But once you touch true love—once you touch truth—you no longer need a system like religion to get you there. The path is clear.

The atom is a good metaphor to help us understand the ultimate goal of religion. An atom includes the conflicting forces of the proton and the electron, which peacefully coexist within the atomic field. In fact, a nuclear explosion occurs when the atom is split. When it is whole, it is immortal. The world has undergone a nuclear detonation for millennia because the spiritual forces have been split into different religions. The key to human immortality is the harmony of all faiths. It is only the ego that causes us to war over our differences instead of celebrating them, preventing us from achieving unending happiness and life.

## THE TRUE PATH

Religion is merely a tool for gaining this clarity. It is not the end but rather the means. The Dalai Lama, the head of state and spiritual leader of the Tibetan people, knows this well. He also understands that religion begins with the heart of the people. When asked about the creation of a world religion, he responds, "We have enough religions but not enough human beings. We need more human beings. Religions should learn from each other, respect each other, but keep their identity. Don't let us talk too much of religion. Let us talk of what is human. Love is human. Kindness is human. Everyone needs love and kindness."

As the Dalai Lama tells us, we just need to get back to basics. And that's exactly what I would like to do now—get back to basics. Religion 101, if you will. By seeing the common threads woven through each of the core religions, we can begin to unravel the layers and reveal the Light beneath.

## CHRISTIANITY

Christianity stems entirely from the concept of love. Jesus taught that love leads to forgiveness and ultimately to a rich, purposeful, and everlasting life. Christianity's core values can be summarized in this way.

*Love.* Jesus emphasized that we should love God and love our neighbor. A story in the Book of Matthew in the Bible makes this clear. The Pharisees asked Jesus to explain which of the commandments was the most important. In response, Jesus said, "Love the Lord your God with all your heart, with all your soul, and with all your mind." In the next breath, Jesus told the Pharisees that the second most important commandment was to, "Love your neighbor as yourself." These commandments are the cornerstones of Christian tradition.

*Forgiveness.* To forgive another is literally love in action. Jesus said, "But I tell you who hear me, love your enemies, do good to those who hate you, bless those who curse you, pray for those who mistreat you. If someone strikes you on one cheek, turn to him the other also. If someone takes your cloak, do not stop him from taking your tunic. Give to everyone who asks you, and if anyone takes what belongs to you, do not demand it back. Do to others as you would have them do to you." These words from the Book of Luke serve as a reminder to Jesus' followers that it is not their responsibility to nurse grudges, but rather to show love and compassion, especially to those who have hurt them.

*Belief in salvation.* Salvation is the understanding that when an individual practices love, that person is led to a life full of purpose and connection to others. By walking this path, a person can be saved or redeemed from the consequences of sins committed in the past. No one is excluded from this promise. Happiness and abundance are available to anyone who desires them.

*Healing and miracles are possible through faith.* Jesus did not take credit for the miracles he performed. Instead, he showed that it was each individual's responsibility to activate healing through their own faith.

*Accept and transform.* God unconditionally loves and accepts every person just as they are, yet he also encourages people to grow and learn from their mistakes. Jesus advised his listeners to live fully and to "taste and see." It is this hands-on approach that will lead a person to spiritual transformation.

## ISLAM

Islam at its core is about forgiveness, caring for those less fortunate than yourself, and equality among all people. Mohammed was a prophet; he never claimed to have invented a new religion. He simply described his mission as an attempt to bring Jews, Christians, and Arab people together. Some of the key principles of Islam are as follows.

*Belief in only one God.* The word, "Muslim" means "one who submits." In the framework of Islam, an individual can only submit to one God.

*Forgiveness of others.* In the Quran 42:40, it states, "The retribution for an injury is an equal injury, but those who forgive the injury and make reconciliation will be rewarded by God." In the Islamic tradition, to forgive another is to open a door for God to enter.

*Treat every person as an equal.* Mohammed viewed every member of his community as equal. A person's status or possessions did not make one person more or less valuable than another. Equality remains a valued Islamic principle.

*Care for those who are less fortunate.* Mohammed took a clear stand on how those less fortunate should be treated. He preaches in the Quran that piety is not found, "in turning your face East or West in prayer." He believed instead that it could only be found through giving. He urged followers to give of their wealth to the poor and needy and to make no one a slave.

*Spiritual awakening requires work.* The word "*jihad*" does not mean "war." It actually means "a struggle," "a striving," or "a great effort," meaning the struggle of the soul to overcome the obstacles that block the path to God. And war, according to the Quran, is never holy.

## BUDDHISM

Gautama Buddha is considered the primary figure in Buddhism. Although a prince by birth, he later went out on his own to experience a life without luxury or indulgence. What he discovered was Enlightenment, and his teachings became an exploration into suffering, the reason for it, and how to remove it. His teachings encompassed the following fundamental principles.

*Belief that there is a cycle for the soul.* Buddhists believe that people are reincarnated over many lifetimes until they become conscious enough to reach a state of Nirvana.

*Treat all forms of life as equal.* Plant, insect, or animal: a person never knows what form his body will take in the next life, so it is important to see all life forms as equals.

*Treat others as you would like to be treated.* Reciprocity is a fundamental law of the universe. Every action a person takes will result in a reaction.

*Develop your mind.* The art of concentration and meditation is central; Buddha taught it was the pathway to freedom.

*Remain pure and calm.* Buddha taught that by practicing discernment and detachment, a person will experience Enlightenment.

## JUDAISM

Like Islam and Christianity, Judaism is based on the teachings of Abraham, and it emphasizes a belief in only one God and the importance of treating others well. In fact, Rabbi Hillel, in the 1st Century BCE, summarized the Bible this way to one of his students: "What is hateful to you, don't do unto your neighbor. The rest is commentary. Now, go and study." The core principles instruct one to:

*Believe in only one God.* God is unique, incorporeal, and eternal. He created humankind in his image and enlisted the help of prophets to share his wisdom and instructions for living with others. To this end, God delivered the Written Torah and Oral Torah to Moses, the greatest of all prophets.

*Do good deeds.* People are inherently good but can lose their way. God knows both the thoughts and deeds of men; nothing goes unseen. Judaism also teaches that God rewards good and frowns upon evil, making it our responsibility to uproot evil that exists among us. This idea is reiterated throughout the Book of Deuteronomy.

*Proactively work to better yourself and your life.* What a person does is more important than what a person believes. By actively following the commandments of God, you become closer to Him.

*Believe the Messiah will come.* Judaism teaches that a savior will come to unite humankind and create global peace, and we should never lose faith in this promise.

*Know that the dead will be resurrected.* In the Book of Daniel it is proclaimed, "Multitudes who sleep in the dust of the earth will awake; some to everlasting life, others to shame and everlasting contempt." The belief that there is more to come after our physical death on Earth is a central theme in Jewish tradition.

## HINDUISM

Hinduism is different than other modern religions in that it does not have a single founder or central religious system. Instead, it is comprised of thousands of religious groups that have evolved in India since 1500 BCE. Some scholars believe that the stories of Jesus were actually inspired by the life of Krishna, a quintessential deity in many Hindu traditions. Here are the key principles of Hinduism.

*All reality is unified.* The universe is one, and this oneness is known as Brahman. There are three parts to this force: (1) Brahman, the Creator; (2) Vishnu, the Preserver of New Creations; (3) Shiva, the Destroyer.

*Your actions in this life will affect you in future lifetimes.* Hinduism supports the idea that there is a continuing cycle of birth, life, death, and rebirth, as well as an accumulated "karma" of good deeds and bad deeds.

*There are four goals in life.* These include: (1) *kama*: sensory gratification in the form of mental, sexual, and other physical pleasures; (2) *artha*: material and social success; (3) *dharma*: spiritual righteousness; (4) *moksha*: liberation from suffering, which is the supreme goal of humankind.

*Tolerance of other religions.* A common Hindu saying is, *"Ekam Sataha Vipraha Bahudha Vadanti,"* which means: "The truth is One, but different sages call it by different names." Hindu teachings recognize the multiple pathways to God and encourage respect among religions.

## WE ARE ALL ONE

How could the loving, enlightened principles articulated by each of these major religions have the power to tear humanity into so many opposing sides? We've gotten too far from the source, that's how. The problem is that the further we get from the Creator and love and tolerance—that is, the source of everything—the more challenging it becomes to see the big picture. The more we interpret this and dictate that, the muddier the original message becomes. Religion becomes convoluted and the original purpose is lost entirely. What began as a system for bringing people together and closer to the Creator has turned into multiple systems that more often than not drive people apart.

When you go to your temple in Jakarta, Indonesia, or your church in Little Rock, Arkansas, it's not easy to see how they are connected, is it? Churches, temples, mosques, cathedrals—they all seem such separate structures, both physically and spiritually. But they are not. At the source, we are one. We are all intimately connected, and because of this fundamental connection, we carry with us a responsibility to our larger global community. The human body exists only through the grace of a network of diverse organs, each one profoundly different than the rest in terms of look, design and function. The body of humanity operates in identical fashion. The terms Israelite, Hindu, Christian, Buddhist, and Muslim merely refer to different vital organs. Our greatness and our success lie in our unity and our diversity.

When we forget about this critical diversity, we open the door to large-scale suffering. For example, the ongoing civil war in Sudan has displaced millions of people and killed hundreds of thousands more.

Starvation, brutality between brothers, sexual violence against women and children, destruction of homes and entire villages—the suffering that exists in this one country alone is unimaginable. What is even more shocking is that religion plays an important role in Sudanese culture. Sudan is comprised of Muslims and Christians, as well as devout followers of other religious systems.

How can religion and extreme violence coexist? If a Christian were truly connected to Jesus, he or she would simultaneously feel an unbreakable bond with Jews, Muslims, Buddhists, and all of those who come from the same source. The same goes for a Muslim who feels unity with Mohammed and a Buddhist who strives for oneness with the universe. If we are truly connected with God, our love for one another is overwhelming. We cannot help but be of service to one another. The idea of committing murder or inflicting pain is impossible!

Even in the finer details, there are resounding similarities amongst religious texts. Scholars stand in agreement on this point. Professor and Christian youth minister Dr. Hugo Schwyzer explains, "All religion is rooted in the tension of wanting to encourage people to transform, while at the same time telling them they are loved as they are. Every religion tells a story between people and the Divine." Gordon Darnell Newby, author of *A History of the Jews of Arabia*, said of Islam and Judaism in the 7th century, "[They] operated within the same sphere of religious discourse." Religious scholar Reza Aslan explains, "Both sides shared the same religious characters, stories, and anecdotes, and both discussed the same fundamental questions from similar perspectives, and both had nearly identical moral and ethical values." Take the story of The Binding of Isaac, which appears in the Book of Genesis. In the Hebrew Bible, God asks Abraham to sacrifice his son Isaac on Mount Moriah. But in the Islamic version of this story,

Muslims believe that God's command to Abraham was to sacrifice his older son, Ishmael, not Isaac. But when we argue names, aren't we missing the point? What does it matter which son was bound? The point is that both stories reveal a similar lesson.

The stories are in fact only slightly different. According to both variations of the story, it is Abraham's steadfast resolve to obey God's command that leads to the positive outcome. After Abraham finishes binding his son to an altar, an angel of God stops him at the last minute, at which point Abraham discovers a ram caught by its horns in the nearby bushes. Abraham then sacrifices the ram in the place of his son. Similar stories of Mary and Amina provide another example. In the Book of Luke in the Christian Bible, Mary hears the voice of an angel that says, "You will be with child and will give birth to a son, and you are to give him the name Jesus." This is notably close to the story of Amina that is told in the Quran. When Amina becomes pregnant, she too hears a voice. The voice says, "You are pregnant with the Lord of this people, and when he is born, say, 'I put him in the care of the One from the evil of every envier; then call him Mohammed.'"

In fact, the stories of the three faiths of Abraham (Judaism, Christianity, and Islam) are so close that in Chapter 3:84 of the Quran, it states: "We believe in God and in that which has been revealed to us, which is that which was revealed to Abraham, Ismail, Isaac and Jacob and the Patriarchs [of Israel], as well as that which the Lord revealed to Moses and to Jesus and to all the other prophets. We make no distinction between any of them; we submit ourselves to God."

We submit ourselves to God; that is the way to happiness. The details of names, dates, and places fall away when we get that it is the lessons that truly matter. I consistently find value in the books of other religions that I read. Why couldn't a lesson from Jesus be valuable to an Arab? Why can't a Jew follow the teachings of Mohammed? Why isn't a Christian able to follow Buddha's pathway to peace and Enlightenment? Why must religions "own" their lessons? The lessons of our greatest leaders were meant for everyone. They weren't meant to be coveted and used against one another.

If Christians who criticize and fear Muslims actually read the Quran, they would know that it includes the fundamental characters in almost every biblical story. Moses, for example, one of the most dominant figures for both Christians and Jews is mentioned over 140 times! But most people don't even read their own literature, let alone the texts of another religion. Without ever having investigated the source material, all too often people beat the drum of war or denounce another religion—actions based on sheer ignorance. But there is a way to obliterate ignorance: by shining a bright light on humanity. That Light is the wisdom of Kabbalah.

## KABBALAH IS JUST A WISDOM

A short time ago, I traveled to a peace conference in Madrid that King Abdullah of Saudi Arabia had called together with Juan Carlos, King of Spain. Upon my arrival, the conference administration had trouble deciding which religion to "classify" me under. The Jews didn't want me to sit with them. The Christians didn't think I belonged. The Muslims were not sure. Eventually, I ended up in my own category, but in truth, I am a Kabbalist. "What is a Kabbalist?" you might ask. It is someone who desires to develop a relationship with the Creator, and does so in two ways: by restricting ego and by developing a greater capacity to share with others.

Kabbalah doesn't fit into any existing religion because it's not a religion. It is wisdom. You can go to a mosque, church, or temple and practice any religion and still be a Kabbalist. Kabbalah is a technology that helps to awaken the soul. It is not a doctrine or set of rules. It is a way of thinking about and understanding the universe, as well as our role in it. Hundreds of years ago, people understood this, but due to the extremism that has infiltrated many religions, Kabbalah has been labeled "mystical Judaism." But when we look at the origins of Kabbalah, we see that this label is misleading.

In fact, the *Zohar*, the source of kabbalistic wisdom, was first translated from Aramaic into Latin, not Hebrew and Pope Pious was the one who suggested and supported the printing of the *Zohar*. The power of the *Zohar* crosses many boundaries. In early 1991, one of my father's students happened to be close to Moroccan King Hassan II and arranged for my father to visit the holy sites in Morocco. Because King Hassan II was a descendant of the Prophet Mohammed, he was also the guardian of the country's holy sites of Islam. As timing would have it, my father happened to be with the king on the eve of the first Gulf War. Knowing that the king had a connection to Sadam Hussein and seeing an opportunity, my father asked King Hassan II to call Sadam Hussein and ask him to give up Kuwait in order to avoid war.

Although the King did call Sadam Hussein, he wasn't able to reach him. He began to explain why he wasn't fearful of the impending conflict. He showed my father a piece of parchment paper that he said had been passed down through each direct descendent of the Prophet Mohammed. When the King showed the sacred paper to my father, he was surprised to see that it actually depicted the *72 Names of God*, one of the key tools described in the *Zohar*. Although it is a mystery exactly how the *72 Names of God* became a sacred document that was handed down through centuries of royalty in a Muslim country, it comes as no surprise that people in different religions and diverse cultures recognize its power of protection and transformation.

## GIVING OVER OUR POWER

We all have an inherent ability to connect directly to God. However, over time people have abdicated this ability in favor of connecting to a priest, rabbi, or some other intermediary. In doing so we have given away our personal responsibility to question, grow with, and connect to the Light. Sure, it may be easier to have someone decide things for us and tell us what to do. But when we give away our power we create separation between ourselves and our source. We cut ourselves off from our own growth and transformation, from our own efforts towards happiness. Now our failures become someone else's fault, and a reason to become victims. We become hardened in our thinking, extreme in our opinions, and intolerant of others and their beliefs. The further we drift away from doing the spiritual work ourselves, the more corrupted the path becomes. Over time, the translators of the source—the rabbis, the priests, and the leaders of countries to whom we give our free will and power, alter religion to suit their own needs.

History is awash in people who have used religion to get what they want. In 325 C.E. the Roman emperor, Constantine the Great, called together the Council of Nicaea to attain consensus on the writings of Christianity. His motive was not love for the core values of Christianity. Rather, after conquering several diverse neighboring lands, he needed to create a unified ideology in order to maintain control and power. In doing so, he took the liberty of eliminating the gospels and passages that could threaten his domain. Another example is when the Pope, the head of the Roman Catholic Church, wouldn't give King Henry VIII a divorce from Katharine of Aragon, the King broke from the Roman Catholic Church and formed the Church of England.

Power-hungry people have and will continue to exploit religion and humanity. So why would we ever choose to put another in charge of leading us down the path to God? Furthermore, what would make us believe that another human being could fix us or absolve us from our wrong turns, our mistakes, and our character defects? The movie *Godfather 3* does a great job of demonstrating the insanity of this way of thinking. After all of the murders and crimes for which he is responsible, the character Michael Corleone simply goes to the Pope for absolution. With one visit, his slate has been wiped clean. Right? Wrong!

If we do not fix ourselves, no other human being can give us absolution. We must do our own dirty work; no one else can do it for us. The only way to correct our negative actions is to transform the inherent selfishness that lies within us—that part of us that the sages refer to as the *Desire to Receive* only for our own interests: We must pull it up by its roots and transform it into something positive. When we start thinking of others, we return to the underlying truths of all religions—love, unity, care, and responsibility for one another. We have to feel the pain that our selfish actions have caused, so that not only will they never happen again, but the selfish motivation for that action will also be transformed. That is how we take control, not over others but over our own negative qualities. This is the true meaning of taking back our power. We change ourselves, and then the entire state of the world begins to change.

## DISCOVERING GOD FOR YOURSELF

As Rav Ashlag explains in *The Book of Introductions*, religion is the work that we do; it's a tool that we can use in order to know God. The Creator has been concealed in order to give us the opportunity to find Him.

In the Middle Ages, the world was ruled by kings, czars, and monarchs. People didn't have access to technology and the abundance of information we have today. They had to accept much of what they were told—not only because it was the only information available, but also because questioning the beliefs and religion of their leaders was punishable by death. There was little room for a person to seek out his or her own path to happiness. Either you were a member of a certain religion or you were not. There was no middle road.

The road that did exist was not an easy path. In fact, suffering was seen as a way to God. The more pain a person could sustain while on this earthly plane, the more he or she would be "rewarded in the blissful afterlife." But suffering is not necessary to reach God. In fact, connecting to God is the path to complete fulfillment, which is the purpose of life and Creation—we are supposed to be fulfilled and perfected. Connecting to God helps us do this—not the other way around. Suffering isn't necessary to finding God; God is necessary to discovering a life free of suffering; God is necessary for happiness!

Religion as it stands today usually suggests something along these lines: Read a particular text, pray several times each day, confess your sins, and attend services of your church, mosque, or temple regularly. And then—if you're lucky—you can connect to God. The end goal, most religions preach today, is to find God. But God isn't the end goal; fulfillment is.

As we said earlier, when we look closely, the five major world religions have more in common than not. In fact, if we put Buddha, Moses, Jesus, and Mohammed all in the same room, they would likely become fast friends. So why the wars? Why the suffering? Because we have bowed out of our own spiritual work. We have stood by and watched as greedy people took the power that we gave them and used it to exploit and destroy. This is the consequence of our benign neglect.

The Israelites acted in the same way. They depended on Moses to free them from slavery. He led them on a journey through the desert and all the way to Mt. Sinai. While they set up camp Moses climbed to the top of the Mount, where he received two stone tablets inscribed with the Ten Commandments. According to the sages, these tablets were not meant to become the basis of a religion for the Jews, but were simply tools to achieve a direct connection to the Creator. That connection would result in total fulfillment, perfection, and immortality for all of humanity. However, while Moses was away the Israelites began to panic. Worried that he might not come back, they melted down their gold jewelry and cast it into the form of a Golden Calf to create a new intermediary to God—and to replace Moses.

The Golden Calf and the orgy that took place are usually the scene-stealers of this story. What is often overlooked is the fact that the Israelites were acting out of fear. They did not want to carry the burden of connecting to God on their own shoulders. The calf and the orgy were simply a way for them to give over their power so that they would not have to be responsible for themselves. Or choose for themselves. Or restrict their selfish ways by themselves. Or share of themselves.

They were unwilling to do what needed to be done. That was the true "sin" of the Golden Calf. And we commit this sin every time we seek someone to show us the path or make decisions for us, instead of making our own direct and pure connection to the Light of the Creator.

Connecting to God is the responsibility of each person. However, we would much rather blame someone else for our misery than to take responsibility for our happiness. The problem is that when we give away that responsibility to someone else, we lose sight of our larger global community. We close off our minds, and this is what makes it possible for us to justify wars, murders, and suicide bombings. Because if we really thought about it and understood it, could killing really be justified in the Name of God? Could destruction really be the path to our own fulfillment? Can hatred really help me love myself and reach my own potential?

The energy we are connecting to when we practice religion is not the Light of the Creator. The god of organized religion is only a frail, jealous, and fearful image mankind creates in an attempt to wrap up the secrets of the universe in a nice, clean package. But the package is not neat and tidy. In fact, the god of religion has become more Golden Calf than God. The Creator has gotten lost in the shuffle of greed and ego.

## THE REAL GOAL IS HAPPINESS

When God gets lost so does happiness—the one true goal of humanity. That's because God is the direct pathway to happiness. We need God in order to experience true fulfillment. I am not talking about short-term gratification here. I am talking about fulfilling the promise of immortality by doing the spiritual work required. When we do not make fulfillment our top priority, we create darkness, and we are not the only ones hurt by our decision. The entire world experiences darkness when we stop making happiness our individual goal. To live a happy, fulfilled, and purposeful life every day is not just a dream; it is our *daily* responsibility.

We do have support in this process. We're not in this alone. There are spiritual laws to guide and teach us: The Law of Cause and Effect, Sharing with Others, and Restricting the Ego are principles that can lead us to fulfillment, if we apply them.

In truth, our soul is always guiding us to the people we should date, the friends we should have, and to those situations that will lead us to perfection and fulfillment in our lives. But we have to make the individual choices ourselves. Ultimately, the journey leads us to understand that the only way to *true* happiness is feeling the pain— and the pleasure—of others, and to truly share their experience. Most of us run from other people's pain—believing that we cannot handle it. We also take little joy in other people's happiness. But we are equipped to handle both.

## 1 + 1 MILLION = 1

One of the greatest misunderstandings of this world is that if we add someone else to our lives, the burden will become more than we can handle. But believe it or not, the more pain you take on from others, the lighter your load actually becomes! Carrying other people's problems, feeling their pain, and caring for them will generate more of a connection to the Creator than praying, fasting, confessing, and meditating combined.

If we feel wiped out when we help someone else, that's a sign that real sharing has not taken place. There is a hidden agenda at work somewhere. Real sharing is like sharing the flame of a candle. By lighting another candle, we do not diminish the original flame; we only make the light brighter and stronger. If we are truly sharing, whether we help one or one million, we never lose or diminish ourselves in the process. It is judging others, jealousy, and the negative thoughts that we experience when we bring people closer that weaken us. Not the sharing. That can never weaken us. The math may not add up in the way you are used to, but it works nonetheless. No matter how many people we choose to share our Light with, we are still as bright as ever before. We are still whole. In fact, we are greater than before, because now we are not just one candle but the cause of many lights.

So sharing Light actually gives birth to more Light. Imagine one candle in a dark room. How much power does that one candle have in the face of all that darkness? But if that candle proceeds to light hundreds of candles not only does that one candle stay intact but now there are hundreds of candles to banish the darkness. The following story of two friends demonstrates this principle in action.

*The Apple Thief and the Shopkeeper*

There once was a king who ruled his kingdom with an iron fist. And he had good reason. A vast number of his subjects were utterly corrupt. They were ruthless scoundrels who were only in it for themselves.

One day, a man by the name of Nathaniel was caught stealing an apple. Nathaniel was not really a bad person, and it wasn't his nature to steal from anyone. But after living among so many villains for so many years, he simply gave in to his selfish instinct on this one occasion. Unfortunately, he picked a bad time to make a mistake.

The king decided to make an example of Nathaniel in order to send a message to the rest of his people, so he sentenced Nathaniel to death. Nathaniel accepted his fate without any fuss. After all, he had no one to blame but himself.

When the king asked Nathaniel if he had a last request, it turned out that he did. He asked if he could have three days to settle his affairs. Nathaniel wanted to pay off some debts, return a few personal favors, and say good-bye to his friends and loved ones. He figured he could tidy it all up in three days.

The king, impressed by Nathaniel's quiet acceptance of his fate and by his sense of responsibility, wanted to accommodate this last request. But there was an obvious problem. "If I grant you this temporary reprieve," the king said, "I have no assurances that you will ever return to fulfill your sentence."

Nathaniel understood the king's dilemma. "I have an idea," Nathaniel responded. "Suppose I arrange for my best friend to stand in for me until I return. If I am late, you can execute my friend in my place." The king laughed. "If you can find someone who will volunteer to take your place, I will grant you your three days. But if you are even one minute late, your friend will be hung from the gallows."

Nathaniel asked his best friend, a shopkeeper by the name of Simon, to stand in his place. Simon and Nathaniel were like brothers, and Simon said he would be honored to offer his life in return for Nathaniel's temporary freedom. Simon was imprisoned while Nathaniel prepared to hurry off and wind up his affairs. "Remember," the king commanded. "One minute late and I will hang your best friend."

One day passed, and then two more, and as the appointed hour approached, still Nathaniel did not return. The king ordered Simon to the gallows and had the hangman's noose slipped around Simon's neck. The hangman tightened it, and a hood was put over Simon's head.

Just then, a rider and his exhausted horse galloped up. "Stop! Stop! I have returned!" It was Nathaniel. "Please, I beg you," Nathaniel cried to the king. "Remove the noose. This is my fate, not his."

But the king replied, "You are five minutes late."

Nathaniel was so out of breath he could hardly speak. "Let me explain, Your Majesty. I was set upon by a band of robbers and barely managed to escape. That is why I am late. It is I who should die. Not my dear friend."

As the hangman removed the hood from Simon's head, he began to shout, too. "That is not true. I am the one who should die today. The king gave his word that if you were even one minute late I would die in your place. Besides, I could not stand living without you, my best friend. But that is not the point. You were late. So according to the arrangement, it is I who will die today."

Nathaniel's eyes welled up with tears. "I beg you, Your Majesty. Do not listen to him. Do not let my best friend die. I could no more live without him than he could live without me. It is I who was originally sentenced to death, not Simon. I beg you to get on with my execution."

The king, not surprisingly, was taken aback. In a land rampant with thieves and villains, the king was not accustomed to seeing such selfless acts of unconditional love. Nevertheless, a decision had to be made. Justice had to be meted out according to the law of the land as dictated by the king.

"I have reached a final verdict," the king said. "Neither one of you shall die. I see that no matter which one of you dies today, I will still be killing two men. The original sentence called for only one man to die. Thus, I am forced to set you both free." Recognizing the greatness of these two men and the power of the bond between them, the wise king asked if they would consider taking him on as their friend.

The love between these two men was so selfless that each was willing to give up his life for the other. Furthermore, their love for one another transformed the heart of a king. How many of our relationships are that selfless? More typically we enter into relationships seeking something for ourselves. We seek approval, acceptance, and happiness from others, and in doing so we create relationships that are unbalanced. But when we truly give to others with no strings attached, we are not diminished, but rather we are made whole. And the more we give selflessly to others, the larger the whole becomes, the more fulfilled we feel, and the more Light we carry with us.

There is another story about a great sage who lived a life full of good deeds and sharing. He was renowned for his generosity and his ability to live without ego. When he died suddenly, he was surrounded by angels who immediately brought him to the Garden of Eden in recognition of all of the good he had done in his life. Upon arriving, however, instead of relishing in his new paradise, he could only feel the pain of those of his friends who were not in the Garden but were suffering in Hell.

Unable to think of anything else, he asked that the angels take him to Hell. Once there he pleaded with the angels that his dear friends be granted their freedom. The angels denied his request and insisted that he return to the Garden of Eden. The sage refused and said he would not leave until every soul in Hell had been released.

The angels could not stand to watch such a righteous man suffer so they asked God if they could make a deal: Each person whose pain and regrets the sage could fully feel would be set free. Over and over again, the sage went through the depths of Hell and experienced horrible suffering as he got in touch with each person's painful burden, while the angels tried to convince him to return to Heaven. However, he refused to leave Hell until the last of the souls were released. When he finally went to Heaven, he rejoiced, knowing that all his friends were there with him.

This is what I mean when I speak of sharing—it's a giving of oneself that may be painful in the short-term but ultimately leads to unimaginable happiness and satisfaction. Yes, when the Light is ready to come, it will feel like a pressure cooker—uncomfortable at a minimum, agonizing at its worst. But it's a temporary discomfort and one that is essential to our spiritual development. Rav Ashlag says that in order to move to the next level spiritually, we need pain. But religion gone wrong undermines the importance of feeling the pain of other people, it numbs us to their suffering as well as our own. Its rules and doctrines encourage us to believe that we are different and separate from one another. It makes it possible for people to engage in war and mass destruction with little or no remorse.

Think about it. Can your body feel good if your foot is green from gangrene? Can your mind be clear when your stomach is in pain? Can your body run a marathon when your heart is broken? We are all a part of one humanity, one body. Just as a hand looks different from an eye, a Hindu may look different than a Catholic. But we are all one and the same. We are all equal parts of a larger whole.

The *Zohar* explains this in detail how each language of the world creates a unique channel for the Light. Furthermore, every nation reveals a different and necessary aspect of the Light of the Creator. Every part of this world exists for a reason—and each nation brings a unique gift and purpose to the greater whole. When we attempt to destroy each other, we seek to destroy aspects of the Light that the Creator has deliberately put into place. As Rav Ashlag explains, every nation, every country, and every culture must exist because each reveals a vital aspect of the Light.

I used to collect baseball cards when I was younger. With baseball cards the term "mint condition" means everything. If a card has even the slightest damage, 90 percent of its collectible value is gone. The same is true of this world. If we damage its citizens in any way, we dramatically reduce the value of the Light that the Creator gave us. The Creator's master plan includes a world that exists in mint condition—unblemished, harmonious, and intact.

Everything that is in the universe, good or bad, has a right to exist, and we have no right to destroy it. But we do have a responsibility to heal it. Healing means to return something to its God-given state of perfection. It is our job to heal whatever needs healing by infusing it with our own Light, our own goodness.

Prayer is one way we can begin the healing process, a notion that now even science has begun to support. David R. Hodges, an assistant professor at Arizona State University, analyzed 17 major prayer studies. The results of his analysis support the power of prayer and its ability to positively affect patients. My belief is that when we take the time to selflessly care for others, in this instance by offering kind and healing words, we exercise the power to change things. The Light of the Creator rides along on our selfless words and actions.

## THE BOTTOM LINE

Prayer is one way in which we can take back our power to heal. Another is by questioning the structure of religion as it is practiced today. By questioning the status quo, we move closer to the Creator. And we must walk the path ourselves. No one else can take the steps for us—not Jesus, Moses, Buddha, or Mohammed. They are but channels of the Light. We need to use them as guides, but we cannot ask them to do the work for us. Nor can we depend on a priest, a preacher, a rabbi, or a best friend. They have their own journey to walk.

It is our responsibility to plug into the source, to plug into God, and to make the connection. We allow ourselves that divine connection every time we overcome daily tests and challenges, every time we share selflessly and with no strings attached. It is our job to use the source—to use God—to transform selfishness into happiness and fulfillment. This is our sweet harvest after all of our hard work in the fields.

# CHAPTER THREE

# IT TAKES A VILLAGE

Our environment is in bad shape. Of course, this is not a new or mind-boggling revelation. It's pretty clear that we have created a lot of damage over time. What's even worse is that we *continue* to destroy the world in which we live. With so much evidence of depleting natural resources, toxic waste, global warming, and irreparable harm to our food chain, why do we keep perpetuating the problem? Why do we continue marching to the same alarming beat?

This isn't the first time I've spoken out on the topic of the environment. I've even written a book on it. But for the purposes of this book, I want to go at it from a different perspective—not just from a kabbalistic point of view, although I will draw on that as well. My goal here is to better understand how we, the human race, got to this point. Why are we sticking our heads in the sand when there is so much work to be done? This isn't about a particular region or country, or about a political party dropping the ball. The environment doesn't belong to any one country or a state, nor does it belong to a CEO or the President. It belongs to all of us. Choosing to build the environment up or tear it down takes a global human effort—and it happens as the result of numerous events that take place within the confines of the human brain.

The adult human brain—the neural hub of pleasure and pain, decision and indecision, self-seeking behavior and altruistic action—weighs about three pounds, but its potential is limitless. No end of research has been conducted in hopes of figuring out how this incredible mechanism does its work. One thing we do know for certain is that different parts of the brain have very specific functions. When we look at two areas of the brain in particular, we can learn a great deal about why we humans do the things we do—more specifically, why we often choose to harm ourselves and our environment when we could be healing our bodies and our world instead.

Studies with Rhesus monkeys show that the brain region known as the prefrontal cortex is stimulated quickly when something positive happens or is *expected to happen*, which leads to the release of a pleasure-generating substance called dopamine. But the brain reacts quite differently when it comes to conscious decision-making. An altogether different part of the brain is stimulated when we're consciously choosing one item or task over another. When researchers tracked brain activity in people grocery shopping, for instance, it was the parietal cortex, not the prefrontal cortex, which showed the most activity.

The problem is that dopamine works so fast that its effects can be felt almost immediately, but the decision-making processes that take place in the parietal cortex doesn't lead to an immediate jolt of pleasure. This makes the prefrontal cortex, with its dopamine connection, the more influential of these two areas of the brain, for better or for worse.

Oftentimes, it's for the worse because the prefrontal cortex can make us prone to quick fixes and addictive behavior. Consider how frequently we engage in destructive behaviors (smoking, drinking, overeating, or over-anything) even though we *know* that they're harmful in the long run. The pleasure-seeking part of the brain is sucker-punching the part of the brain that has the ability to weigh consequences and make appropriate choices.

The worst part is that all of the time, effort, and money we spend satisfying the pleasure-seeking part of the brain is for naught. There will never be enough money, enough Starbucks coffee, enough food, enough sex, or enough drugs to make us feel truly fulfilled. Your only chance to change for the better is to get far enough away from the dopamine-trigger so that you can see the bigger picture. Only when you step back—way, way back—to see what else is possible, can you move away from quick fixes and instant gratification.

The time is now. Not only is our relentless search for pleasure at all costs destroying our bodies, our relationships, and our wallets, it is wreaking havoc on the world in which we live. We are so strung out on temporary highs that we are failing to weigh the consequences of our actions on ourselves and on our environment.

When we look at all of the publicity and the marketing campaigns for making the world "greener" and compare them to what people are actually doing (or not), the discrepancy is huge. But now that we know how influential the prefrontal cortex is, the story becomes a little clearer. We don't act in the environment's best interest because feeling good now is far more important.

Let's get real here. Even if hybrids were the cheapest cars on the market, everyone would *still* not run to buy one. Hybrids don't fulfill that short-term spark of dopamine that we get from sexier, flashier, or more prestigious cars. In order to change our way of thinking about the environment, a deeper change has to happen within us. Until we step back to see the larger picture of global health and our role in it, we will not step up to the plate to change the direction in which the world is heading.

Consider the following.

Yat Sun, based out of Hong Kong, is one of several companies that sell shark fins in the South Pacific region where shark fin soup is considered a delicacy. The demand for shark fin soup is so great, in fact, that conservationists claim that more than half of the world's sharks are under threat of extinction. Unfortunately, however, the fin is the only part of the fish used. Fins are cut from live sharks that are then left to die in the water. When Hong Kong Disneyland first opened, it added shark fin soup to its menu, against protests from activists. However, Disneyland refused to withdraw the item. Its justification was it felt that it needed to show respect for Chinese culture. Ultimately, after a global email and letter-writing campaign, Disney finally removed the soup from its menu. Since then, concerned environmentalists have since been using the momentum gained from their Disney success to persuade hotels, grocery stores, and restaurants to stop selling any product that contains shark fins.

This victory aside, the demand for shark fin soup remains strong. Eric Bohm, Chief Executive Officer of the Hong Kong World-Wildlife Fund (WWF) said of the Disney success, "Regretfully, it's a drop in the bucket. The trade in shark's fin is absolutely huge—it's mind-boggling. Thirty to forty million sharks a year are being harvested."

Until consumer demand diminishes, a supplier will always be willing to step in. The motivation to change this cycle has to begin with a change in the way the public *thinks*. Ultimately, there has to be more perceived benefit associated with the conservation of sharks than with the taste of a savory bowl of finely prepared shark fin soup. This change seems hard to imagine in light of the power of a dopamine buzz. But we have seen situations where masses of people *did* make a decision to serve the greater good of their community rather than succumb to the allure of short-term pleasure or monetary gain.

In their book *Sway*, authors Ori and Rom Brafman share a story about a town in Switzerland. When the townspeople were originally polled about becoming one of two regions that would house toxic waste from a new nuclear energy program, 50.8 percent of the respondents agreed. They were willing to put themselves at risk for the greater good of the country's people. However, when the local government attempted to increase that number by paying people off, the number of supporters for the toxic site dropped by half. A majority of the townspeople in Switzerland had enough conviction about their obligation to the community that even money (usually a key dopamine trigger) could not influence their decision. In fact, introducing money into the picture actually cheapened the project and made it seem less socially motivated and motivating.

As a society we must get to a point where temporary pleasure doesn't offset the irreversible damage we are causing. Unfortunately, people usually require a major wake-up call before they will give up behaviors that drive a dopamine addiction. Most smokers quit right away when they get a reality check—in the form of a malignant tumor. Overeaters keep eating until they suffer from a heart attack, stroke, or diagnosis of diabetes. Sometimes we have to hit rock bottom in order to wake up.

What makes this even harder is that we humans are remarkably adaptable. For those readers who live in Los Angeles, let me ask you how many times you step back and really notice the smog? People who visit the city are appalled by the murkiness of our skyline. But those of us who live here have become so conditioned that we don't even notice it!

In order to change *anything*, we have to fully associate with the long-term effects of the actions that we take rather than the highs of the moment. We have to be able to feel that the consequences of our actions are more painful than a brief pleasure. Or as my mother, Karen Berg, always taught, we have to get to a place "where the pain of not changing finally becomes greater than the pain of changing."

Global transformation must come from a profound shift in how we think and, therefore, how we act. All of the government-based incentive programs in the world can't create lasting change. Think about it. Giving energy companies and chemical manufacturers government funding in the hopes that those same companies will, in turn, treat the environment with more respect can't make a difference where it counts. It will not affect the core values of the person whose livelihood depends on that company—especially if it's a business that has been there for generations. Manufacturing pesticides, burning coal for energy, mining mountaintops—these are more than just things we do; they are jobs, lives, and identities. That is why moving closer towards sustainable ways of living requires real transformation—

transformation that must take place in our very roots. Anything less is a top-down approach that will offer nothing but temporary gains.

Change *is* possible. The key lies in looking at the bigger picture. Before a company is asked to change its product or services, it needs to be prepared to determine how its business can fit into a new global vision. The same is true not just for companies but also for individuals, communities, cities, states, and even entire countries.

Turkey is a great example. This is a country that was encouraged to change by a power greater than dopamine. What has more power than pleasure? A common vision and the clout to support that vision. The world's leading countries threatened to cut Turkey off economically if it didn't take care of the country's addiction to opium during the 1970s. The decision that Turkey eventually made to eliminate the entire opium industry would be like Colombia eliminating the cocaine trade today. It was an enormous undertaking that changed the dynamics of an entire culture—and its future.

President Richard Nixon assisted in the transition. During a public statement, he explained how difficult it was for Turkey's leader, Prime Minister Nihat Eram, to make this decision:

*For hundreds of years, tens of thousands of Turkish families have raised the opium poppy as a legitimate cash crop and for its edible oil and seed. Under a United Nations convention, Turkey is one of those few nations permitted legally to grow poppy for export. Yet Turkey is one of the few opium-cultivating countries in which the use of opium or heroin as an addictive drug is virtually unknown. Since the opium farmer has little if any knowledge of his part in the spread of a frightening international epidemic, a ban on opium production is a particularly difficult decision. These circumstances accentuate the vision and wisdom of this very important step. We know well the importance of the agricultural sector of Turkey's economy, and we are prepared to put at the disposal of the Turkish government our best technical brains to assist Turkey's program to bring about a better life for the Turkish farmer. We are proud to assist in a program from which we all will benefit.*

Imagine how this approach could affect some of the issues our world faces today. Many of these challenges currently exist in Afghanistan. This is where terrorists are being trained and educated, where women are being oppressed, where the Taliban has taken their power to an extreme, and where opium is the currency driving decisions and creating conflicts. Today, Afghanistan is the opium leader of the world. In 2007, 90 percent of the world's opium came from this region. More land is currently being used in Afghanistan to grow opium than is devoted to coca in South America. But it could change, like Turkey, if the catalysts of a common vision and the leverage to support that vision are brought to bear.

## GUARANTEED DESTRUCTION

Imagine if there was no oil in the Middle East. What would the world look like? Many of the challenges we are facing would simply disappear. Greed is the driving force behind so much destruction, war, and death.

We can't continue like this. If we keep walking this well-worn, mindless path, we are guaranteed destruction. But we can't change by taking our usual approach. Quick fixes and band-aid approaches will get us nowhere. We have to go about things differently this time. As Albert Einstein famously said, "You can't solve a problem with the same consciousness that created it."

It's impossible to avert our eyes to the mounting evidence against us and what we have done. As global citizens we are witnessing an increase in air pollution, soil erosion, and dust storms that cause lung diseases and leave families without basic sustenance. We are experiencing an increased number of natural disasters such as earthquakes, hurricanes, cyclones, fires, and mud slides. While some parts of the world are suffering long-standing droughts, other communities along coastal areas and rivers can no longer escape deadly floods during their rainy seasons.

We can't escape the consequences of our actions—or inaction. Not dealing with problems can lead to the same costly consequences as direct, harmful action will. When the nuclear reactor at Chernobyl exploded in 1986, the news that the Soviet government broadcast to the world was unclear at best. It admitted that a catastrophe had occurred, but the rest of the facts came slowly. As a result of the government's lack of transparency, people in the immediate vicinity were exposed to unnecessary health risks. Some sources estimate that the total deaths related to the Chernobyl disaster may grow to more than 4,000. Others say that even that number is low.

In the case of Pacific Gas & Electric (made famous by Erin Brokovich), when the company found out that their facility was responsible for contaminating waterways in Hinkley, California, with cancer-causing hexavalent chromium (otherwise known as "Chrome 6"), PG&E officials chose a quick fix instead of immediately ceasing production of the toxic by-product and finding a safe alternative. They attempted to remedy the problem by secretly buying and destroying all of the property near waterways affected by the pollutant. Clearly, when large amounts of money and a system that seems too daunting to change are at stake, many business and government leaders choose to become secretive or just look the other way instead of finding workable solutions.

With so little real change taking place, the outlook can seem hopeless. Sometimes it feels as though we will have to destroy the entire infrastructure on which we have built our lives in order to start over. One thing is for certain: We must look at the seed—the source of every one of our thoughts and actions. When the seed is "caring for thy neighbor as thyself," everything that springs from it will be good. But even if the original idea *seems* harmless, if selfishness is at its core, it will eventually lead to destruction.

From 1900 to about 1935, big cities in the United States mostly relied on trolleys for public transportation. Because they generated no carbon dioxide emissions, these trolleys were environmentally friendly long before the phrase was ever a buzzword. Over time, however, transit owners were lobbied by groups such as General Motors to introduce buses as the main means of transportation. The sell was pretty easy, as buses were less expensive to buy, required less maintenance in terms of rails and infrastructure, and the sheer novelty of the bus substantially increased ridership rates. With returns as obvious as this, no one stopped to think about the long-term consequences of elevated $CO_2$ emissions. In fact, the federal government actually created a big advertising campaign to introduce buses into the community.

Once again, the insatiable corporate appetite for a quick buck (or millions of bucks) precluded a thorough assessment of the situation. And of course any time we talk about fast money, quick fixes, and short-lived pleasure, we are talking about dopamine. This is what drives consumer demand, which in turn drives new inventions, corporate supply, and the greed machine.

Of course greed is not just limited to big business. It exists anywhere people are acting out of self-interest. During a long-running government attempt to persuade several Native American tribes to allow the nuclear power industry to use their reservations as a dumping ground for waste, the U.S. Congress ultimately created the Office of the Nuclear Waste Negotiator in 1987. This office targeted an additional two dozen tribal councils for waste sites. Although the government dissolved the office in 1994, the nuclear power industry jumped on the trend and continued to offer compensation to tribes for their land. One such tribe, the Goshute Indians in Tooele, Utah, took the bait. As a result, companies such as Envirocare and Magnesium Corporation have been dumping voluminous amounts of chlorine gas and radioactive waste into the region, which many believe has adversely impacted the health of tribal members.

As one tribal elder put it, "The real issue is not the money. The real issue is who we are as Native Americans and what we believe in. If we accept these wastes, we're going to lose our tradition." If we want to experience profound change, it must start at the core: our beliefs, our thoughts, and our actions must be parsed and analyzed closely. We must put what we believe ahead of the gratification of a quick buzz. When we uproot the self-seeking component we uproot destruction. We uproot greed. And we start the ball of transformation rolling.

## THE POWER OF COMMUNITY

To change as a global community, we need to understand what "community" really means. Before industrialization, when we all lived in an agrarian society, people had to work together to survive. Communities were built around supplying the basic needs of the people who lived there. Everyone depended on one another for food, water, fellowship, and transportation. This is what it meant to be a part of a community.

We also need to take a closer look at the word "environment." It's a word that has taken on a very specific connotation in recent years. It has become an object worthy of our protection, something essential to creating a "greener" world. However, environment also describes the area around each of us, as well as our immediate experience. In his simple yet profound manner, the great Kabbalist Rav Ashlag explained that environment means "surroundings." Surroundings. Community. Environment. They are all really one and the same. So how we choose to treat our surroundings/community/environment will have a seismic impact across the globe. Yes, this ripple effect starts with us as individuals, but it will also impact all of humanity. And humanity is our ultimate community.

The idea of community has become complicated in the modern world. Sure, when we go online to a social networking site it might feel like we are a part of something; we might even call it our "community." Facebook. MySpace. Twitter. By the time this book is printed, there will probably be a new online community that is hip to join. The problem lies in the fact that we have no responsibility in these groups. We can simply plug in when we want, and hit "sleep" when we are done. In some cases, instead of truly connecting, we have actually created disconnections. The world has become smaller and bigger all at the same time! The best part of today's online community is that we can be connected practically *anywhere*. We have an amazing opportunity to unite the world, and yet we are all still locked into our own limited realities where we don't have to deal and change. Imagine the potential we have at our fingertips if we learn to use technology to create *true* connections among people—connections in which we feel responsible for one another. Connections that make us feel full instead of leaving us wanting more the minute we log off.

One hundred years ago, it would have been hard to believe the degree of interconnectedness we now experience on the planet. The modern telephone was still a relatively new concept. Television didn't exist. The Internet was decades away from even being an idea. You couldn't just hop on a plane and fly to another country; that was years away from being a reality. A century ago it was hard to imagine that everyone on the planet was really sailing in the same vessel. Few people would have understood—much less believed—the concept of the Butterfly Effect: that a butterfly flapping its wings in Los Angeles could set in motion a domino chain of events that could ultimately lead to an earthquake in Japan. We are increasingly open to understanding how we are all connected, and that if we sink the ship that we are all sailing aboard, we *all* drown. However, we have simultaneously become so focused on our own life experiences that we think we are alone. In the not so distant past, we were close enough to our community to physically see how our actions impacted the group overall. Now it's just too easy to look the other way, or turn off the TV or computer and detach ourselves from others.

But remember that true community is not just about being geographically close to someone. It's about feeling connected and responsible for what happens. If we isolate ourselves in our homes, cubicles, and cars and don't take on a sense of communal responsibility, how can we ever feel connected with others? Every so often it occurs to me that if I didn't live next to my brother, I would not even know who my next door neighbor was! Animals know not to poop or pee where they sleep, but we get into trouble that way because we have created a world where what we don't see does not exist. And it's all too easy to remove those things that are not convenient from our line of sight. We lose sight of the interconnectedness of all things in life, of the relationship between *cause* and *effect* in the environment.

Every function in a working community has value because it serves the group's combined interests. Like the African proverb says, "It takes a village to raise a child." Everyone plays a crucial role. This means we can't create change in a vacuum. You might choose to drive a Prius, but what good does this really do if you are cutting people off while you are driving? What we are starting to understand is that what you do—even if no one sees it—can still harm the community's energy and physical being. The good news is that what you do can also help, especially when it comes from a place of empathy.

It's important to remember that the combined influence and wisdom of a group is more powerful than that of an individual. In his book *The Wisdom of Crowds*, author James Surowiecki explores several cases where group efforts outweigh that of the individual. He cites a story about a group of people asked to guess the weight of an ox. Although many of the individual guesses were far from accurate, *the average guess of the group was only one pound off!* As Surowiecki explains, "Under the right circumstances, groups are remarkably intelligent, and are often smarter than the smartest person in them."

For many decades, the United States has been a world leader, but as the country has become more and more divided, its strength and influence in the world is diminishing. What causes a machine that was once the best to start falling apart? It's simple. Power starts to diminish the minute one part becomes more important than the whole. When one person starts to place his or her own needs above the well-being of the larger group, tiny cracks start to form in a once well-oiled machine. Self-interest undermines unity. It can sabotage even the strongest of unions, the most powerful of communities.

Actions taken in the interest of the self destroy the sanctity of the whole much in the way that a cancer cell affects the body. When one bad cell starts to greedily feed on those cells around it without any regard for its host entity, it destroys the very thing that gives it life. The key is to keep the body healthy so renegade cells can't get a foothold. Being a part of a working, unified community is a stepping stone towards a more holistic and greener future. When you become part of a group that is collectively working to make a difference, change will follow organically.

## WHAT'S YOUR AGENDA?

Because self-interest can be a silent killer, it's imperative to assess your motivation along the way. If our motives are not in line with the good of our community, what we perceive as good efforts can sometimes go very wrong. This is often the case with radical activists who hurt others or destroy property in an attempt to facilitate change. Using the environment as an excuse to further your own agenda does nothing for the greater good of the community. Instead, such actions infuse fear and hate into an already wounded environment.

Sometimes it's challenging to figure out the right thing to do, especially with all the hype around "going green." Take the recently touted use of ethanol to replace traditional gasoline. Ethanol is a renewable, homegrown fuel made from corn that has been proposed as a way to help lower the United States' dependence on foreign oil. However, as more and more ethanol is made from corn, less and less corn is available for food production. A study conducted by Iowa State University researchers reported that U.S. ethanol production could consume more than half of the country's corn, wheat, and coarse grains by 2012. Costs will be driven up for acreage, food, and livestock production, leading to increased global food shortages. Rapid growth in ethanol production has already substantially raised U.S. food prices and impacted the price of corn tortillas in Mexico, inciting protests.

The California Air Resources Board indicates that ethanol is worse than oil in terms of greenhouse gas emissions. According to the California regulatory agency, corn-based ethanol is far worse in the long run. Washington D.C. says: "If increased production of corn-based ethanol in the U.S. raises corn prices and accelerates the conversion of rainforests... to farmland worldwide... loss of the carbon sink associated with such deforestation and disruption must be counted towards the biofuel's total emissions."

Sometimes even when we think we are working towards viable solutions, we are really adding fuel to the fire. That is why it's so important to look at the bigger picture and to keep examining our motives as we make decisions about our environment. Are we really making choices that lead to a net benefit for our global community?

## BEING A TRUE ACTIVIST/ ENVIRONMENTALIST

In his teachings, Rav Ashlag explains that we lose a sense of community "when the needs and desires of the individual become more important than the needs and desires of the group." The fact that we are all interconnected is not something we readily see. We lose sight of the fact that when we hurt one another we are actually hurting ourselves. When we neglect our responsibilities to the rest of the world, it's like cutting off a part of our own body. We are diminished, and can no longer function properly as we were intended. We have a responsibility to our surroundings—our environment and our community—to become aware and to stop taking more than we give back. When we take without understanding that everything is intimately related, we are making decisions without seeing the entire picture. It's easy to assume that if something is happening in a far away country it's not *really* a part of us because we can't directly see and feel its effects. We may feel bad for the people experiencing the problem, but we don't really internalize their pain as our own.

There is a story about a miracle-worker. Miracles were a way of life for him. His days were spent praying for the sick and meditating on their recovery. One day, he got a knock on his door and the man who stood there asked, "Could you help me? My son is sick in bed. There has got to be a way you could help. Please come with me."

The sage agreed to see what he could do. He followed the man to his home and entered the room of a very sick child. After several hours, he was drenched in sweat from the intensity of his prayers and meditations for the boy. Finally, he told the father, "I'm sorry—I have tried everything. There is nothing that I can do to save your son."

The father was utterly heartbroken. In his pain he took off on his horse and began riding blindly at full speed. Suddenly, he heard a horse galloping behind him. It was the kabbalist. Excitedly, the man asked, "Did you receive a response to your prayers? Will there be a miracle for my son?"

His head bowed, the sage replied, "No, I'm sorry. Nothing has changed."

The man shouted at him angrily, "Then why did you chase me all the way out here?"

And the sage replied, "If I cannot help you, the least I can do is to cry with you."

The two men dismounted their horses and sat on the side of the road together, shedding tears of sorrow and pain over the loss of a son.

Sometimes, when you just don't know what to do or what to say, something as simple as sitting and truly being present with someone can make all of the difference. Maybe it's by making a phone call to someone who needs a listening ear; maybe it's by grieving with another over the loss of a home or loved one. Our job is not always to take away the pain. Sometimes it's just to make sure that another person knows they are not alone—that we are here, too, and can be with them while they feel what they need to feel. This is community.

As the story turned out, when the two men finally returned to the father's house, they found that his child had made an astonishing recovery. There was absolutely no trace of illness left in his body! It's wonderful that the child was spared, but the real message of this story lies in the fact that the sage didn't stop trying to help, even when it seemed there was no hope. There is always something we can do, even if it's just to weep with those who suffer and help them bear their pain.

If we truly understood how the world worked we would know that if something is brought to our attention—if we can see it in our viewfinder—then it's our responsibility to do something about it. We must always do everything we can to influence the situation for the better. We must reverse the trend in the world community of becoming increasingly disassociated from our responsibilities to one another.

A 13-year-old girl in Auckland, New Zealand, sought help moments before she was attacked by a man who had been threatening her. The young girl approached a woman filling her car at a gas station and begged for help, but the woman's response was to tell the girl to "keep away from the man" before the woman drove off, leaving the girl to be assaulted and raped. Can you imagine this?

In another shocking display of avoiding responsibility, a surveillance video caught a car plowing into a 78-year old man trying to cross the street, leaving him crumpled and bleeding in the middle of the street. Incredibly, the driver of the car kept going. Even more disturbingly, the other cars on the street and nearby pedestrians didn't do a thing to help the injured man! The camera footage goes on to reveal nine cars driving by without stopping, as the elderly man lay in the street. More than 40 sickening seconds went by before anyone even stepped off the sidewalk to take a closer look at what had just taken place. Even then no one went over to assist the man or to divert traffic.

Finally, after about a minute and a half, a police car responding to a different call came across the scene of the hit and run and called an ambulance. How have we, as a society, reached this point of dissociation? Rav Ashlag tells us the world was created to give us the illusion of dis-connection. This gives us the ability—the free will—to *choose* selfishness, or its opposite. It provides the opportunity for us to ignore the pain and the good in others without seeing that the real negativity is within ourselves. If we knew that by hurting others—or by not helping them—we were hurting ourselves, we'd realize that the effort it takes to help others is actually self-serving, in a good way. This world was created to give us the illusion of separation so we could chose unity of our own free will.

Consider this true story that took place in California. When "good Samaritan" Lisa Torti stopped to pull Alexandra van Horn out of a wrecked vehicle that she believed was about to explode, her efforts may have contributed to van Horn's paralysis. So van Horn sued Torti, the rescuer. Keep in mind that California has a Good Samaritan Law, a law that was originally created to protect people like Torti who make an extraordinary effort to help a fellow human in a life-threatening situation. But that law was reversed when the California Supreme Court ruled 4 to 3 that Torti was at fault. The case was hotly debated, but the court had the final say.

As a result of this new law, people in California will have to add another layer of worry to the already difficult question of whether or not to step out of their individual life bubbles to help someone in need. The fact that our court system can fault people for trying to help others says a great deal about the state of our society. We have collectively allowed ourselves to get to this point. Instead of naturally letting community happen through our own growing compassion, awareness, and concern, we are continually trying to legislate it. In doing so, we help numb our human responses, avoid our responsibilities to each other, and deny ourselves our true potential to grow as human beings in a global community.

Let's face it, people; we just don't want to deal. We self-medicate to desensitize ourselves or chase short-term distractions, including technology, pornography, drugs, or self-righteous personal agendas. Alternatively, we want to avoid the problem entirely by assigning blame elsewhere, or by denying the problem exists altogether.

There is another way: we can accept the problems we have created, learn from them, and then work together to discover viable solutions. This is the only way we grow as individuals and as a society. Without accepting responsibility or by blaming a particular group, we just keep digging an even bigger hole, and environmental problems become environmental disasters that we can't reverse. We have to deal with both the problems we have created ourselves—even if our own hands didn't dump the chemicals into the waterways or if our own power saws didn't chop down the rainforest. We can't keep suing one another to make the problem go away; we can't continue to bury it underground and wait for the toxins to leach into our communities. It doesn't matter if it's our physical garbage or our emotional garbage that we're dumping. We can no longer hide it from the world. We must deal with it as our extended human body, which it is, or everyone will suffer.

Becoming a true activist—being a true catalyst for change—can only happen when we change ourselves. This understanding opens awareness within us, and once we have this awareness, the universe makes it clear what we need to transform inside. The world is, in fact, a mirror. If we look at the world this way—as a mirror of self—we can direct our efforts and *activism* inward and clean house spiritually. Change will then manifest in the physical world automatically. These elements are the only way to transform selfish behavior. When you think that you are being an "activist," when you're really just stuck in a personal agenda, you are actually creating a problem that is even harder to solve than the issue you are fighting!

Because we're all connected, nothing outside of us will change until we change ourselves. We tend to want to "change the world" in order to make our lives better. Instead, we need to change ourselves in order to make the *world* better. It's a paradox. The more you want to change the world, the more you have to change yourself.

Consider this story about Mahatma Gandhi. A woman brings her son to Gandhi, complaining that the boy eats too much sugar. She wants Gandhi to tell him to stop. Gandhi asks the woman to bring the child back the next month. The woman has traveled too great a distance to be able to return home, so she stays nearby for a month, at some hardship and expense. The following month she brings the child back, and this time Gandhi says to the boy, "Stop eating sugar, child." And the boy does. The woman is pleased but puzzled. Several days later, as the woman prepares for the long journey home, she visits Gandhi with a question. "My child has done what you asked, but why could you not have said those words the first time I came?" "Ma'am," Gandhi replies, "a month ago I was still eating sugar."

Mahatma Gandhi knew that we can't very well advocate something that we ourselves are not doing! Or, as Gandhi famously put it, "You must be the change you wish to see in the world."

## THE BLAME GAME

When we activate change from the inside out, we are implicitly saying no to playing the blame game. We are saying no to playing the victim by taking responsibility for ourselves and for the world around us. At times we've all pretended that the bad things in the world don't directly affect us, but such denial is as harmful as the problems themselves. Others of us are clearly involved in the problem, but instead of standing up for ourselves and our community, we sometimes take on the role of the helpless victim. But neither denial nor ignorance is a valid excuse—not ever. We are all involved. All of our choices matter. Every one of us plays an important part in every outcome.

Ultimately, as Rav Ashlag explains, problems in our world exist for two reasons—because of the person who creates the problem and because of the person who *allows* it to happen. We always blame the perpetrator, but rarely if ever do we take a look at the victim. The people who are closest to a problem (and who eventually become directly affected by it) usually have an opportunity to change course, or direction, at a seed level. However, if the opportunity is not taken before the damage begins, those who had the power and position to change things end up becoming perpetrators of their own suffering.

In February of 1946, Commodore Ben H. Wyatt, the military governor of the Marshall Islands at the time, traveled to Bikini Island. One Sunday after church, he assembled the native Bikinians to ask them if they would be willing to temporarily leave their island so that the United States could begin testing atomic bombs for "the good of humanity and to end all world wars." You can watch the U.S propaganda video at: http://www.youtube.com/watch?v= Yc_T3nSlg7M. After a very stormy deliberation among his people, King Juda, the then leader of the Bikinian people, stood up and announced, "We will go, believing that everything is in the hands of God."

While the Bikinians were preparing to leave their island, the U.S. Navy gathered a huge flotilla and a massive amount of equipment, including approximately 242 naval ships, 156 aircraft, 25,000 radiation recording devices and 5,400 experimental rats and livestock. More than 42,000 U.S. military and civilian personnel were involved in the testing program at Bikini Island, which detonated two nuclear bombs on the island. A former enlisted Navy serviceman who had contracted cancer had this to say about the fateful events: "There's no question in my mind, that of all the things that went on in *Operation Crossroads*, it was a slow death from that time to this date. Not only for me but for thousands of men out there that may be worse off than I am. There are so many thousands of those men that are dead now, and they don't really know what caused their death."

Despite the test's extraordinary risk to people, animals, land, and water, thousands of people knowingly stood by and let it happen. Like the perpetrators, those who stand by and allow themselves to be the victims of injustices are equally responsible for the outcome. This is a difficult thing to hear—that men and women who suffer play a role in their experience. It's so easy to find fault in those who cause pain, but it's almost criminal to suggest that those who accepted it are part of the problem. However, as adults, we have choices. If we are the perpetrator we always have the choice of whether or not we will take the action that causes pain; if we are the victim we have the choice of accepting it. Often that choice comes with a perceived sacrifice that we may not want to make, so it's not easy to take responsibility for who you are in the face of what is happening to you.

## THE TEACHER

The only way to effectively do the real work of improving the environment is with a teacher. We cannot do it alone, without someone who challenges and encourages us to make the corrections we need to make in this life. The real value of a teacher is to help us remove our own personal selfish desires so that we can see we are all fingers and toes on the same human and environmental body. We are all connected.

We came here to do some very specific work: to look past our own selfish desires and to share of ourselves. Our goal is to get to a place where we are acting in true service to one another, no matter our circumstance.

A true teacher is not someone who advises and lectures. Finding a teacher is not about seeking wisdom—we can find wisdom anywhere. A teacher is someone who keeps us motivated to change, someone who keeps our desire burning in order to help the world. Rav Ashlag explains, "The purpose of the study, the purpose of our spiritual work is to come to a point where we actually have a physical sense, a physical taste of the Light of the Creator."

When Rav Ashlag first met his teacher, he went through many stages before he connected to the Light and truly understood their relationship. His first obstacle was that his teacher seemed to have a huge ego. Rav Ashlag could have simply walked away when he first made this observation. However, he chose not to judge his teacher, but to listen to what he had to say, and to believe that something deeper would be revealed. Craving the wisdom, Rav Ashlag continued to meet with his teacher. But instead of sharing information and revealing the secrets of the universe, his teacher continually told Rav Ashlag what was wrong with him. Despite this, Rav Ashlag continued to seek out and work with his teacher.

He began to realize that the goal of all of the work that we do in this life is to purify ourselves, which can only come with a greater awareness of our inherent *desire to receive for the self alone*. In fact, Rav Ashlag's teacher told him, "If you are growing in your uncovering of this great ego that you have, you are growing. If you are not, forget about anything else."

Although his teacher sometimes seemed close to revealing a great secret, Rav Ashlag always left his lessons with a sense of yearning. His teacher constantly left him hungry for more. But through this process Rav Ashlag learned that self-satisfaction and self-contentment breed ego. When his teacher passed away, Rav Ashlag still felt unsatisfied. He said, "I cannot express in words the tremendous pain that I felt. My hope was that my teacher was going to reveal to me, and elevate me to the level of one of the great souls that ever lived—and I was left with nothing. Not only did I lose all hope of ever gaining more wisdom, but everything that he had ever taught me from the pain and the loss—I lost it all."

However, Rav Ashlag didn't give up. Even when he was at his lowest, he realized that he had to continue his own studies. "From that moment on, I looked up to heaven and I awakened a tremendous amount of yearning." Eventually Rav Ashlag realized that his teacher had helped him to become a channel for the Light. When he realized this, he also understood that this gift was directly linked to the Creator. He said, "How can I even thank the Creator? The Creator knew all along how little I have, that I don't have understanding, I don't have enough Light and wisdom to give thanks for the great gifts, certainly not to earn them, to deserve them. But, of course, the Creator chooses whoever He chooses to be His revealer of Light."

Because of Rav Ashlag's decision to keep returning to his teacher and to listen to what he had to teach him, he was given a divine gift from the Creator. That's how our teachers help us to grow. They awaken within us a desire to be more, to know more, to push further than we ever would on our own. One of the reasons that high school athletes can now break Olympic records set in the 1920s is the power of their teachers. Coaches now analyze physical movements down to the smallest detail. Golf coaches can suggest the minutest alteration to a swing, swimmers can review extensive video footage and a detailed overview of every stroke: coaching has become unbelievably systematic. A good player says, "I missed." A great player says, "If I would have done this *one* little thing differently, I would have got it." And what makes it possible for us to find and understand that *one* little thing that makes all the difference? A teacher. No one is above needing a teacher, even though we forget this sometimes. Unfortunately, instead of finding someone worthy to guide us, we sometimes fill that role with celebrities, would-be gurus, and people with their own agendas.

A worthwhile teacher can determine why you make certain choices and take certain actions. He or she can pinpoint subtleties in your nature that you cannot see yourself, and a good teacher will go to great lengths to accomplish this. Rav Brandwein, who was my father's teacher, had a difficult time teaching my father because Rav Brandwein's family was opposed to it. Even when Rav Brandwein was on his death bed, his family wouldn't let my father near him. After Rav Brandwein's passing, my father felt great despair, but then Rav

Brandwein started to come to him in visions and dreams. My father would ask him questions and he would answer.

One night my father went to sleep asking his teacher if it was right for him to teach Kabbalah to the woman who would become my mother, Karen. Today the idea of teaching someone Kabbalah seems like nothing, but at the time, this was an historic and monumental departure from the tradition of Kabbalah, in which these teachings are the exclusive province of men. My father received no reply and interpreted this to mean that the answer was no.

However, when my mother met with my father later that day she told him about a strange dream she'd had the night before. "A man who I've never met before came to me in my dream, and when I looked at him, he put his hands over my head. He said something to me in what sounded like Hebrew, but I didn't understand him. When my father asked my mother to describe the man, she described Rav Brandwein in great detail, including his clothing. "He was dressed in a long coat and carried a cane. And, he had a big fur hat on his head," she said, all of which was unerringly accurate.

Although Rav Brandwein could not spend as much time with my father in physical form as he wanted to, that didn't stop him from being my father's teacher. Not at all. He literally died in order to make a real difference for my father, and that is what makes him a true teacher. He was willing to sacrifice everything for his student. It should be noted that it's an unusual occurrence to have a teacher in spirit. It's safe to say that it's a special kabbalist and a special teacher who experience such a nontraditional classroom!

Ultimately, in order to grow to achieve our purpose and take responsibility for our lives, our community, and our world, we need a teacher in the physical world who can constantly push and challenge us until finally… we become teachers ourselves. This is the last step in the path of becoming one with the Creator. As the 11th century Kabbalist Solomon Gabirol explained, "In seeking Wisdom, the First Stage is Silence, the Second Stage is Listening, the Third Stage is Remembrance, the Fourth is Practicing, the Fifth is Teaching." However, you cannot just *decide* that you're ready. Only your teacher can tell you when it's time.

After Rav Brandwein had been studying Kabbalah for a number of years, he asked his teacher if he was ready to teach. His teacher informed him that he was not yet ready. After the 1929 stock market collapse, Rav Brandwein lost his job as a bricklayer, but he finally found work as a garbage collector. He went to his teacher and told him about finding the job and asked him if he should take it. His teacher, Rav Ashlag, responded, "Now, you are ready to teach."

Rav Shlomo once sent one of his students to see a great master who was very old. He felt that the wise old master might have something to share, but he didn't know what it was. So Rav Shlomo instructed his student to go without providing an explanation for the visit.

Upon his arrival, the great master immediately asked the student, "Who sent you?" Feeling that he could not be untruthful, he answered honestly: "Rav Shlomo."

"Go back and tell him that I remember when we were together with the Seer of Lublin," (a great sage held in high esteem by the sages). Shocked, the student said, "That's impossible. My master was four years old when the Seer of Lublin passed away."

The next day, the student came back. Again the great master asked him, "Who sent you?" Again, the student replied, "Rav Shlomo." Again the master replied, "Tell him I remember when we were together with the Seer of Lublin." Again the student left frustrated.

This happened for the next three days. Finally the student gave up, and headed home. Upon returning, he reported to Rav Shlomo, "I'm sorry, but the great old master must be losing his mental acuity. He wasn't making any sense."

Rav Shlomo said, "Tell me exactly what he said." When the student told him the story about the Seer of Lublin, Rav Shlomo began to weep. When he had recovered his composure, he told the student about a time when he was three years old, and had gone to attend a wedding with his father. Sitting high on his father's shoulders, he had watched the newly married bride and groom exit down the aisle. Following them was the Seer of Lublin, accompanied by his student, who would become the old master. When they came abreast of Rav Shlomo's father, they stopped. The Seer of Lublin grabbed the tiny hand of the three-year-old Rav Shlomo and said, "This child will grow to become a great teacher and great leader."

Rav Shlomo cried, "I can still feel him holding my hand. It's clear to me that this message reveals a great blessing. It's time for me to become a master myself."

When we pay attention, we receive cues from the world around us, telling us what next steps we need to take and clarifying our responsibilities in this world. However, these cues must also be accompanied by constant reminders to keep moving forward. These come from a teacher and from a community that respects us and our work in order to provide the fuel needed to continuously progress.

## LOVE THY NEIGHBOR

We know that the greatest revelation of Light in human history took place on Mt. Sinai. My father, Rav Berg, says that what was revealed was the Light itself and with that revelation it became clear that the destiny of humankind was immortality—life without death. While the sages say that indeed this great wisdom was revealed to Moses that day, in truth, the revelation was actually even greater than was reported. Even more significant than the Light and wisdom that was brought forth is the fact that what happened on Mt. Sinai was the result of the divine power of community.

Before Moses went up the mountain he made the Israelites commit to each other that they would all love their neighbors as themselves. Each would be the cause of his or her security and happiness. (It's important to note here that the Israelites represented all souls that come to this world: black, white, Christian, Muslim, Asian, European, you name it; the Israelites were all of us.) Moses emphasized that the revelation could not happen unless the Israelites made this promise. So every person agreed to take care and work for every other person, and to fulfill each other's needs and desires as if they were their own. At that moment, they all become responsible to each other forever. There was no agenda, no selfishness, and no one was left feeling needy or hungry. This was the first true community.

Rav Ashlag once examined social systems in relation to human nature and the creation of critical mass within a society. What he discovered is that the consciousness of the masses is what creates change. In other words, we have within us enormous transformative power when we are working together as a whole. This can work for us or against us. We do things together as a group that we would never do as an individual; peaceful moms and well-dressed dads can turn into raving lunatics at their kids' soccer games, for example. This has been described as "group consciousness." Look at the groups you belong to. Your sports team, your friends, your drinking buddies, your work friends, your Facebook friends—these are your communities and as such they have collective power. Each community has a momentum all its own.

Rav Ashlag explains that we are each part of a community, even if we don't always understand that we are, or act like we are. Think about your life. Whether it's in your workplace, your gym, your book club, or your night club, you have a part to play. And whatever direction those groups are moving in is the direction you're moving in too. The choice we have in the matter is what group we choose to be involved with. Once we have chosen the community, the set of friends, or the partners, the wheels are set in motion and it's incredibly difficult for one individual to change the group's course. Therefore, we should look at our lives carefully and realize that there are people in our communities that might be bringing us down. We have to step back and realize that whether we like it or not, whether we agree with it or not, we will be affected by them.

Our community is essential. If we work hard at correcting our nature but are not a part of an environment that supports and nurtures us, there will be little energy to sustain progress. What we need is to find the same love that the Israelites had for each other on Mt. Sinai—a love so great that it allowed the revelation to take place. If we can accomplish this, we can completely transform the world. If 18 people can bring terror to the United States and the world as they did on 9/11, imagine what a great community of Light could do?

What happens around us is caused by our own actions—and by who we are. If we see selfish people, it's because we are selfish ourselves. When we experience catastrophes, when we see our world's resources becoming depleted, we have to look at ourselves. Our plight is a direct result of not loving our neighbor as we love ourselves. We've been taking far more than we have been giving.

We don't have to look beyond ourselves to fix the world around us. The answers will unfold the moment we start fixing ourselves on the inside. Once we align our lives with solutions rather than problems, we can contribute that power to a like-minded, supportive community. Then the pace of the miraculous starts to quicken. What's more, the answer will never seem as weighty as the problem; the solution will seem simplistic! That is how the universe works. Darkness is complicated; Light is simple.

Think about this: There is a scale that is evenly balanced in the world. Every catastrophe has a 50/50 chance of occurring. It's our own actions that tip the scale one way or another. In every single moment we have a choice: to work on ourselves and create Light, or to let the world tip towards darkness. It's up to us. It's up to you.

Find a community that serves you. Find a teacher who will challenge and help you to see more than you can see about yourself. Stop your addiction to those things that won't serve you or your community in the long-term. Make this your mantra: "When I change myself, I change the world!"

# CHAPTER FOUR
# SMOKE & MIRRORS

It seems harder and harder these days to get a handle on what money actually is. Sometimes it seems like nothing more than numbers in a computer. Most people don't carry cash anymore—I don't even own a wallet! The entire financial system acts like a complex illusion— smoke and mirrors—and yet every digital dollar spent creates changes and quantum effects that we are not aware of. Our present economic crisis shows just how much we have lost touch with the energy of money and how it is meant to be used.

In our world all energy is in a state of equilibrium, and money is a source of energy that affects that equilibrium. Every nanosecond our monetary actions trigger countless little energy shifts. It's like the earth's tectonic plates—they are constantly in motion and any number of small factors could combine to trigger a large-scale event, such as an earthquake or tsunami.

If you look closely at the way most of us conduct our lives, 80 to 90 percent of our days are focused on making money—not making things or providing services, but making money. We spend so much time and energy chasing after money, yet we spend very little time looking into how we and others are affected by our actions—we're often not even aware of what we are *truly* selling, or how we are producing it. Consider some professional services that seemingly contribute to society but upon closer inspection turn out to have profound hidden costs for our lives, our bank accounts, and our world.

Enron is a prime example. This Texas-based energy company was considered a huge success story for many years. It turned out, however, that although Enron was run by some of the smartest people in business, their company was only a success on paper. According to the documentary film *The Smartest Guys in the Room*, the only reason for Enron's extraordinary success was its skill in developing new accounting tricks so that the company *appeared* to be a top performer.

Overall, the company's leaders were not focused on providing a service that would benefit society, but on creating the illusion that they were "New Economy geniuses" who could successfully enter any line of business and become profitable. By taking the standard accounting practice of creating "special purpose entities" to new heights of complexity, Enron was able to increase its leverage and return on assets without having to report debt and losses. Investors bought into Enron's sleight of hand for years until the corporate shell game was finally revealed, and the resulting tumble in the value of Enron stock dealt the company a mortal blow.

Smart corporate and private investors alike also fell for Bernie Madoff's Ponzi scheme—a hedge fund that consistently reported 12 to 15 percent returns. In reality, Madoff didn't invest anything, he simply kept all the money that was given to him for investments and used it to purchase boats, houses, and other personal luxuries. Whenever investors requested money Madoff would pull the amount requested, plus the so-called interest, from his pool of other people's investments. Think about it: smart, highly-educated, financially savvy people gave him $65 billion, over almost two decades! When a major European bank investigated Madoff's firm in 2003 they found so many red flags that they put Madoff on an international black list and advised their clients against giving him their money. However, they then proceeded to invest $10 million Euros of their own money with him!

The aspect of this story that leaves experts around the world still scratching their heads is why didn't anyone ask more questions? If it is our natural tendency *not* to trust people, how did so many trust Bernie Madoff with so much? It seems that when faced with the prospect of fast money, we let our guards down and make decisions that we would never otherwise make. The appeal of easy money is too tempting to pass up, especially when a crowd of other investors are doing the same thing.

We have become so obsessed with making money that we have forgotten its real value and the fulfillment that comes from the effort it takes to earn it. Few parts of the so-called developed world really *make* and *sell* anything any more. We trade digital money for intellectual property in a long-running numbers game.

## ALL FOR $10 JEANS

Another aspect of disconnecting from our money is that we don't realize the power our choices have when we decide how to spend it.

As consumers, everything we buy affects the global economic system. For example, with consumerism as our guide we seek to "have it all," whether we can afford it or not. The lending crisis, brought on by lending institutions who gave out loans to people who could never pay them back, is the macro story, but on a micro level how many of us go to a discount store to find discounts that allow us to have the goods we want at a "price we can afford," like a pair of $10 jeans? We don't ask *how* the jeans could be sold for the price of two Starbucks coffee drinks, or think to question who is being short-changed in order to make this bargain possible. Usually we don't even care—we're simply happy to save some money and to have a decent pair of jeans to wear.

Unfortunately, the reality behind what it takes to offer those jeans at such a low price might not make us so happy. Although many discount stores have similar policies, let's look at the most dominant in the market—Wal-Mart. The company's founder, Sam Walton, put in place a business model that Wal-Mart still follows. Their objective is to dominate the retail market by cutting prices, thereby increasing sales volume and driving other local retail stores out of business.

The result of their hard-nosed competitive practices means a loss of local businesses and individualized customer service, fewer product choices for consumers, and an increase in sweatshops that produce more goods for less.

A June 2007 report by Students and Scholars Against Corporate Misbehavior investigated Wal-Mart's auditing procedures of five Chinese toy factories and found that the factories were going to great lengths to conceal labor abuses. The report noted that "managers conducted 'training sessions' with workers on how to answer questions from Wal-Mart's auditor inspections. At these trainings, managers warned workers, 'If you answer auditors' questions incorrectly, we lose orders and you lose your job.'"

In another such investigation, the United Kingdom newspaper *The Guardian* newspaper interviewed eight workers from seven factories in Bangladesh. All but one of them claimed to work 12-hour days and sometimes through the night to finish an order for Wal-Mart. The workers were paid eight cents an hour—a wage that was not enough to support their families.

Although these examples may sound appalling, you and I have to take some responsibility for these oppressive working conditions. First and foremost we purchase the $10 jeans to feed our consumerism without looking beneath the surface to find out *how* these jeans could be sold so cheaply. What corners were being cut? Who was forced to forego fair pay? We keep our eye on a short-term prize and disregard the consequences. We need to ask more questions.  As my father, the Rav says, we need to ask, "Why?"

The Japanese have integrated this concept into their business and manufacturing culture by adopting the premise that you need to ask "why" five times before you can allow yourself to think that you have arrived at the answer. The "five whys" method currently used by Toyota helps the company focus on the cause of a problem rather than just the symptom.

In Japan this technique is part of a manufacturing model, but in truth we should *all* be asking *why* on a regular basis. The real reason for asking is to become aware of the bigger picture. Once we do so we will also start to understand that our choices have a quantum effect, that energy is generated by what we do, by what we choose. It is ultimately *our* decision to demand a pair of $10 jeans, which is why Wal-Mart makes them for us.

Spiritually speaking, we have lost touch with the energy in money. It doesn't matter what an economy is built on; if the population loses touch with the value and energy of money, the economy cannot survive in the long-term. If we associated bargain-priced jeans with the fact that a child worked 12 hours to make the jeans we are wearing, made eight cents per hour, and went home hungry, we wouldn't want those jeans. We wouldn't want that energy anywhere near us, much less on our bodies.

There is a story about a king who wanted a new suit. The king bought the most expensive Egyptian cotton available, spending thousands of dollars on all the necessary materials. He gave them to the best tailor in town, who quickly made the suit to the king's personal specifications. However, when the tailor brought it to the king, he disliked the suit so much that he wanted the tailor to repay him all of the money he had spent.

Devastated and confused, the tailor went to see the wise man who lived across town. In tears, the tailor explained his predicament. The sage reflected for a moment and asked to see the suit, which the tailor brought to him immediately. He looked at it for a moment before responding, "I see your problem. While making this suit, you were thinking only of the money you were going to make and the cost of the materials. If you unstitch the suit and make it again while only wishing good things for the king, you will be fine."

The tailor took the sage's advice and re-stitched the suit, putting all of his energy into good thoughts about the king. When he brought the suit back to the palace, the king proclaimed it the most beautiful suit he had ever seen. The fabric, materials, pattern, and craftsmanship were all identical to the first suit. The only difference was the energy that the tailor put into it.

We should all care about the energy in the clothes we wear and the food that we eat. Whether we are aware of it or not, the energy in everything we consume or wear affects our lives and the larger economy. Just think about how much the value of money has inflated over the years. A dollar used to mean something. Several hundred years ago $300 could buy you a nice piece of land; now it buys you a pair of designer jeans at full retail.

Money has power, and we are meant to use it to generate true fulfillment and to create lasting, real wealth for everyone. As the following story illustrates, the energy in money can be light or dark, depending on where it came from and how we use it.

There once was a very simple man who worked hard, saved his money, and eventually became proprietor of a small pub. The unusual thing about this pub owner was that he had a reputation for wisdom, so people often sought him out for advice in solving their problems. It was said that his blessings were so powerful that he could even resurrect the dead.

Curious about his uncanny abilities, one of the townspeople asked him his secret. He said, "One day I decided that I needed to connect only to positive energy. I take care of all the people who work at the pub, I make sure their families are cared for, and I make sure only to hire people who I appreciate and who appreciate working with me. This is what gives me the energy to provide blessings and channel positive messages for others."

Think about this story for a minute. The man who was always connected to positivity could have decided to use that energy only for himself, but instead he did *everything* he could for himself *and* for others. This gave him the power to be more than just an ordinary man.

A partnership with positivity is what is missing in the world's economy. As Rav Ashlag explained, in order to be (and to remain) successful, we must have both a connection to energy and to a higher purpose. What that means in practical terms is that it's not all about me; it means that there is something more at play, a grander scheme, a universal system of cause and effect. We are empowered when we realize that our choices have consequences for better and for worse and that they affect everyone, not just ourselves.

## DIG DEEPER—SMALL ACTIONS HAVE BIG CONSEQUENCES

We cannot just take things at face value without doing our homework. For every "simple," "fast," "easy" small action, there is always a larger context. Everything we do carries a hidden price tag: there is the labor required to create it, as well as its effect on our energy, our health, and our planet. All man-made items are part of a web of planetary effects that we don't see without digging a little deeper.

For example, there are people who routinely make a habit of buying clothes, wearing them for a particular event, and then returning them.

In the clothing industry this behavior is known as "wardrobing," and it costs retailers about $11 billion annually. This is money that stores could use to invest in ways that would benefit consumers. Perhaps it could pay for more workers, increase quality in manufacturing, or lower prices for everyone, stimulating the economy. If I buy a suit to wear to one event and then plan to return it, I may think to myself, *I am just one person borrowing one suit.* But this is the way that a lot of our small problems become big problems; we may think we are only one person performing this action, when in truth we are part of a human family of six billion people. It doesn't take long before our actions can, in effect, create a plague. We don't know how powerful we really are; we don't realize that even our smallest actions have consequences too.

As consumers, we have to be mindful about our purchasing behavior; as individuals we have to understand that we are powerful and we have responsibility for the world we live in—and that includes our economy. Every small action we take with our money, whether it's shopping consciously or thoughtlessly buying foods that harm our ecosystem, becomes something much larger and more global than ourselves—for better and for worse. Each of our actions stimulates exponential change. Once those actions reach critical mass, they trigger actions from other people in other places. This is how the quantum world works.

The word "quantum" comes from Latin, meaning "how much," and refers to the units of matter and energy that were predicted by and observed in quantum physics. In the realm of quantum physics, experiments have established that the mere act of observing something actually influences the physical processes taking place, and that the information involved moves instantly across vast distances.

Quantum energy and information is at work while you read these words. Whether you are a scientist and you call it quantum physics, whether you are a Buddhist and you call it the Dharma, or whether you're a Christian and you call it God Consciousness, there is an energetic dimension that influences and is influenced by our every action. Everything we do is added to the global balance sheet. If a tornado of negativity arises, we can choose to be part of it or we can choose to counter it. Although we believe we are alone and powerless, we are mistaken. The Universe is always watching and taking our actions into account.

Part of the kabbalistic legacy is a story of the great sage, the Baal Shem Tov, which brings home this point.

One day there was a knock on the door at the Baal Shem Tov's house. One of his students opened the door to find a shabbily dressed beggar man standing outside. The student offered him a few pennies and started to close the door, but the man insisted on talking to the Baal Shem Tov. The student tried to dissuade the man, telling him that his master was very busy, but the beggar was adamant. Then from within the house, the student heard the voice of the Baal Shem Tov, who said, "Let him in."

Upon meeting the Bal Shem Tov, the beggar told him this story. "Twenty years ago, I was the wealthiest man in town. I had everything. I had mansions, servants—every luxury imaginable. And then one day I lost everything. Everything. Not just money or power. Everything that was important to me was suddenly gone. Why? What happened?"

The Baal Shem Tov asked the beggar, "Do you remember the day that everything changed? You were walking from your house to your factory, and you ran into a man in the street whose belly ached from hunger. He asked you for help. You had plenty of money in your purse, and an apple in your pocket, but you didn't even give that to him. You just kept on walking. That man, who never ever did any harm to anyone, was dying, and you passed him by. Even the angels in Heaven—who have seen a lot in their immortal lives—were horrified: *How dare this person to whom God has been so generous be so completely insensitive to the pain of a man on the verge of death?* And so they decreed that the tables be turned, and that everything that you had should go to this starving man."

The homeless man was in shock. He asked, "Is there any way for me to get it back?" The Baal Shem Tov replied, "Yes, there is one way. If you ask the formerly starving man for something and he says 'no,' then everything will return to the way it was before. He'll go back to being a beggar, and you'll go back to your former life of luxury."

Armed with this insight, the beggar set off for the wealthy man's home. He knocked on the door and asked, "Can I have some money?" The wealthy man answered, "Of course." He took out a few rubles and gave it to him. The next day the beggar went back and asked, "Can I have an apple?" And the wealthy man answered, "Of course, here is an apple." He went back again and again and each time the wealthy man gave him whatever he asked for. Now the beggar was becoming terribly frustrated, so he decided to take a more aggressive approach.

The beggar returned to the wealthy man's house at 3 a.m. and knocked on the door. The wealthy man answered, "Yes, can I help you?" When the beggar asked, "Can I have some water?" he said, "Sure." He gave the poor man water. The beggar returned again at 5 a.m. and again at 11 p.m. Every time, the wealthy man gave him whatever he asked for.

Not long after this, the beggar discovered that the wealthy man's daughter was getting married. The beggar figured that at the wedding of his own daughter surely the rich man would be so busy that he would refuse the request of a beggar. The wedding day came and the ceremony was performed. At the reception, the father started dancing with his daughter. In the middle of the dance, the beggar ran up to the father and asked, "Can you give me 50 rubles right now?" And the father looked at his daughter and said, "One moment." He stopped dancing, took out his wallet, and gave the beggar 50 rubles. At which point, the beggar realized that he would never get his life back from this man. There was no limit to his goodness and his generosity.

The point of this story is that the universe is always watching. With one seemingly small action, you could lose or gain *everything*.

## PICK YOUR POISON

Some of the largest and most powerful industries are in the addiction business. Alcohol. Drugs. Tobacco. Sex. These industries are supported by those who purchase their products or services, as well as by governments that depend on their tax revenue. There is no question that individuals, companies, and governments know these addictions are not good for people. We are all aware of the destruction they cause to our health, relationships, and overall wellbeing. However, we continue to contribute to the problem.

We blame the tobacco industry for producing cigarettes. We blame drug cartels for producing cocaine and heroin. We blame pimps for the sex trade. But the truth is that if there was no consumer, the seller would go out of business. We cannot rely on the government to stop the problem; in fact the government often makes it worse. What we are talking about here is not the cigarette business, the war on drugs, the issue of pornography, or the traffic in sex slaves—what we are talking about is the exploitation of addictive behaviors to make money. As with most wars, we are fighting the wrong fight.

In 1971 President Richard Nixon declared that fighting drugs needed to be a major priority for the United States and the world. More than 30 years later, the former presidents of Brazil, Colombia, and Mexico announced that it was time to replace the War on Drugs with a more realistic, humane, and effective drug policy. The three men concluded that, "to be effective, the new paradigm must focus on health and education—not repression."

Since the War on Drugs began, over $500 billon has been spent on the fight. Sadly, the United States Drug Enforcement Administration (DEA) has little to show for its efforts. Cocaine is as prevalent now as it was 30 years ago, not to mention cheaper and more pure. And as a result of the war on cocaine, methamphetamine, hardly used 15 years ago, is now used by an estimated 1.5 million Americans. The problem is that ever since the war was started, the focus has been on locking up drug users and to attacking the trade at its sources overseas rather than on educating people about the dangers of drugs, decriminalizing drugs, and treating addicts as patients rather than criminals. In the end, only the individual user can stop addiction. Even if we stop using a particular drug, if we don't change our addictive behavior, we will only move on to another form of addiction.

In addition to exercising our power as consumers to make conscious decisions when we are purchasing products, we need to look at our own role in *selling* goods. We need to look closely at our own profession and ask ourselves some hard questions: "Is this serving the greater good? Or am I only serving myself?" It's not an easy pill to swallow, but as long as we seek only to benefit ourselves, we are no different than a pimp or a drug dealer.

In truth it does not matter if we are the dealer or the user, what we need is an opportunity to see the bigger picture of our actions and to take responsibility for making a change.

Batsheva Zimmerman is a powerful and committed woman who travels through the cities and jungles of Colombia sharing Light in some of the darkest places on earth. In her work Batsheva has met many drug lords as well as addicts. The following is her story of Gilberto Rodriguez, head of the Cali drug cartel.

> When I went to visit them, Gilberto and Miguel Rodriguez were in prison. Miguel did not really want to study Kabbalah, but Gilberto did. When I got to his room, his wife was there, as well as a few other prisoners. The energy was heavy and harsh—it seemed that there was no opening for my help. For a second I asked myself, "Why am I here? Why did I come?" I started to speak and they listened to me for about a minute before Gilberto and several other inmates began speaking amongst themselves. I thought to myself this is hopeless—there is too much negativity and darkness here.
>
> But then I caught myself and I realized that I was focusing on the darkness and the ego and not on the soul; that's when I

made a switch inside. I decided that I want to speak to the soul of Gilberto—to his Light! I didn't come here to judge, I came here to give Light and connection to Gilberto. From that moment on, they became silent. I spoke for a while and I realized that the energy in the room was different, and everyone was quiet and attentive. The color of their faces had looked gray before, but now I saw them as a healthy pink, full of energy, and the look in their eyes was alive.

I took the Zohar in my hand, opened it, and gave it to Gilberto. I said, "O.K., now scan the letters and be open to whatever happens." He did it, and then after about two or three minutes he said to me, "Listen, I don't know what this is, but I feel it, I feel it here," and he pointed to his chest. "I feel it here, I feel it, and I want it." He was speaking very brutally, not gently at all, but when I looked closely I saw he had tears in his eyes. Of course at that moment I also got very emotional—there was such a huge switch from being in such heavy darkness to such Light.

When I said goodbye, Gilberto said, "Every time that you come to Colombia, please come and visit me; I want to learn more." And that's what I did. I visited him maybe five times in total, sitting all day with him, teaching him Kabbalah and reading to him from the Zohar. I remember that every time I saw more and more changes in him; he was more open, calmer, and more soft-spoken. I felt that he was going inside himself and was taking more responsibility for his life.

The last time I saw him, he told me: "I know that I did a lot of bad things, and I know it's not the way, and that I need to pay *for this. I am just asking for an opportunity to fix it and to do good to the world." It was a very emotional moment.*

*After Alvaro Uribe became president, Gilberto and Miguel Rodriguez were transferred to another prison and went through a very tough time. The government wanted him to give them information, tell them things, so they made him stay alone for months, without speaking to anyone; they wouldn't let him sleep; it was very hard for him and he was very sick. Then he was taken to a prison in the United States.*

*Two years ago I went to Colombia to give the Zohar to the head of the prison system. Usually I don't tell anyone who I teach, but this time I found myself telling this man about Gilberto, and about the fact that I'd spent time with him and that I'd given him a Zohar too. He said, "What? You gave Gilberto Rodriguez a Zohar?"*

*"Not only did I give him a Zohar," I replied, "but I taught him and his family Kabbalah."*

*He became very excited, and said to me, "Now I understand! Now I understand!! Yes, it makes perfect sense!"*

*He told me that as he was being taken to prison in the U.S., Gilberto seemed like a completely different person—humble and soft-spoken and sensitive. He told those around him that he knew that he had contributed lots of negativity to his country and to the world. He said, "I am asking for forgiveness and I only wish I could correct things; and I really wish I could help; thank you for everything," and he went on the plane. Everyone just stood there with their mouths open and didn't know how to make sense of the extraordinary transformation that had taken place in this previously violent and brutal drug lord.*

I think this is an amazing story of rehabilitation and transformation, and I hope it awakens you to how much power we really have and to what an impact small gestures make. Please refer to this Wikipedia site to learn more about Gilberto: http://en.wikipedia.org/wiki/Gilberto_Rodr%C3%ADguez Orejuela.

If we are given the opportunity to see someone else's pain it is because we have the ability do something about it. If we see someone in pain and we don't do anything, this is the lowest form of behavior, as demonstrated by the wealthy man who angered the angels. We only get to witness that which we can affect. To see is just ego. To help and to be part of the solution is Light.

There is a beautiful story of the Seer of Lublin. He was a great sage who had the gift of seeing things that took place thousands of miles away. He could see not only what was happening in the physical realm, but he could also see inside the hearts of every single person. He could see the good, the bad—everything.

The Seer once had a student who continually pleaded with him, "Please show me just a glimpse of what you see." And the Seer would refuse him saying, "You are going to be sorry if you ever see what I do—it's going to cause you great pain." But the student persisted, until finally the Seer agreed. He brought the student to his study and together they looked out the window.

The student noticed a window opening within the window, and through that window he saw a very wealthy man riding in a carriage. Suddenly a poor man dashed out from the curb and tried to get the rich man's attention. The wealthy man stopped the carriage and asked the poor man, "What do you want, how can I help you?"

The poor man replied, "I have not eaten for weeks, and I am on my way to town. Can you please give me a ride?"

Seeing this great opportunity for generosity, the student said, "Wow, this rich person is going to help out this poor person. That's wonderful!"

The wealthy person pulled the poor man up into the carriage and continued toward town. A few minutes later, when the carriage reached a quiet stretch of road, the poor man took out a knife and began to rob the wealthy man of all his possessions.

The student stepped back from the window, deeply disturbed. "This wealthy man just took this poor person on the carriage and was trying to help him," he said to his teacher. "I don't understand. Why would the poor man rob him?"

The Seer looked at him and said, "I told you this would cause you pain and suffering. Just seeing things accomplishes nothing, which is why ordinarily you cannot see." They continued to look through the window until the Seer said, "The only thing that the wealthy man could do now is to take that piece of wood on the floor there and hit the poor man with it before he is stabbed. I will help him." Sure enough, just as the poor man was about to stab him, the wealthy man grabbed the piece of wood and struck his attacker.

His heart racing, the student exclaimed, "Wow!" To which the Seer replied, "Just to see is worthless, but to see and then do something about it—that is power. Seeing what's inside one's heart while not doing anything about it is pointless. To see pain, hurt, and emptiness, and then fill it with Light—that is worthwhile. The real test of this gift of sight is whether or not you are able to make a difference in someone else's life."

We all have the power to change the world we live in. Every action really does make a difference. From a spiritual perspective, we simply have to stop sleepwalking through life and begin to question what we see, asking the question *why* until we can look deeper to reveal the truths around us. The truth is that small actions matter, that energy counts and affects us all, and that addictions and greed are *our* problem, not just the fault of the industries that profit from them.

Instead of relying on the government, on corporations, or on activists, we need to understand that one little change compounded over the course of time has huge results…or ramifications. One action may seem like nothing, but it's not. The difference it makes may not be immediately apparent, but we have to realize that we can and we do have the power to impact the world around us, and that we exercise that power every time we act, whether we realize it or not.

Start asking questions. Start noticing where you are part of the problem. Start opening up to a higher awareness. When you do, you become part of the solution.

# CHAPTER FIVE

# IT'S YOUR DECISION...

Many spiritual teachings extol the benefits of just *being*. But we did not come here to be, we came here to become: to overcome the destructive beliefs that limit us and to *become* our perfected selves. The challenge is that we get in our own way. More specifically, our fears get in our way. Our fears are the underlying drivers of those limiting and destructive beliefs.

For example, it is fear of being hurt that prevents us from ever experiencing a real relationship. It is fear of being poor that prevents us from finding our dream job. It is fear of being insignificant that keeps us from offering our gift so that we can share with the world. Ironically, it turns out that by giving into our fears, we create the very reality we're so desperate to avoid. Did you ever wonder why people who get attacked by dogs are often the ones who are afraid of dogs?

Although this dynamic sounds straightforward, in everyday life these fears are not always easy to see in ourselves. They are a reactive malfunction built into our DNA, and part of our journey through this lifetime is to become aware of this aspect of ourselves. In fact, discovering our underlying fears is the key to determining what we came here to change; to uncovering our purpose. As if that weren't enough incentive, the longer we remain unaware of this truth about ourselves, the more chaos we will bring into our lives and the further we will get from what we truly desire.

My DNA as a Gemini means that I lose focus and am easily distracted. The underlying fear that drives me is a nagging sense that I will miss an opportunity. Those of you who have read my books or daily tune-ups or have heard me speak know that I discuss this theme often. This is why I answer every email, every text, and every Twitter message. I get thousands of messages every week, and I make a point to check them all; there was no way this book was getting published without a discussion of missed opportunities.

You see, our soul has a built-in navigation system that is designed to put us at the right place at the right time to meet the right people on our journey. It will strategically direct us to the street corner where we will meet our soul mate. Or it will make us miss our flight so that we can catch the next one and sit next to our future business partner. The challenge is that we are not always paying attention to this soul navigation system, so we miss its directions.

This possibility keeps me up at night.

We are often just one person, one phone call, or one step away from the solution to all of our problems. If our soul is always putting us in the right place for redemption and we just don't see it, how painful is that! This completely nullifies the idea that if it didn't happen, it was not meant to be, which is simply a way we make ourselves feel better if we missed the opportunity.

There are many ways that we miss opportunities. The least obvious is that we don't even notice them. Maybe we are too preoccupied with a career, too focused on ourselves, or too busy with an addictive behavior. The point is, for whatever reason, we fail to see what is right before our eyes. Another possibility is that we recognize an opportunity but we choose to run away from it, we choose to take the "easy" way out instead of taking the road that seems more challenging. Sometimes we simply quit instead of rising to the occasion, facing our fears, and tapping into something greater within ourselves.

There is a famous story that is told in many traditions. I heard it in the Yeshiva where I studied, and I think it makes the point crystal clear.

Long ago in a small town in Europe, there lived a young butcher. One night, his deceased father came to him in a dream. The father said, "A woman will come to you on a Friday before the Sabbath. She'll ask that you slaughter a chicken for her. Don't refuse her. You must do as she says."

Many Fridays came and went, but still there was no woman.

Seventy years passed. Then one Friday before the Sabbath, the now old butcher was on his way to temple when a woman approached him and said, "Please, I know it's late, but if you don't slaughter this chicken, I won't have anything to eat!" The butcher looked at his watch, and then shook his head. "I'm very sorry. I'd like to help you, but I just don't have time." And he departed.

140

**THE POWER TO CHANGE EVERYTHING**
CHAPTER FIVE: IT'S YOUR DECISION...

But later that night, in the middle of *Kiddush*, he suddenly remembered the dream he had had so many years earlier and realized he had to slaughter the chicken for the woman he had met. How would he find her? He sprang into action. He told his wife about the woman, instructing her to give the woman food if she ever saw her because he knew that he himself had missed his chance. Indeed, that very night, the butcher left this world. But at least he gained the merit of completing his task through the actions of his family.

We must face it, it is going to happen; we are going to miss opportunities. However, we can minimize these missed chances by fully understanding the spiritual principle of the journey of the soul. We need to train ourselves to become awake and alert to see opportunities for fulfilling our life's purpose. We need to scan our lives for those moments in the same way we have trained ourselves to check our emails and our tweets every day. The next time something happens to you that's a little out of the ordinary, take a closer look for the opportunity it presents.

I am blessed to have people share their stories with me through email. I find this correspondence inspiring, and it keeps me going to know that I have touched someone and made a difference in their lives or given them an opportunity to make a difference for others. Each story is unique, but each one also has a message that can benefit the rest of us. Jemma's is just such a story.

*From Jemma.*

*Unfortunately, I think it takes a tragedy to hit home in order for people to truly take advantage of life. Most of us take it for granted. I was diagnosed with ALS (Lou Gehrig's disease) when I turned 30. Now, looking back, I feel like my whole life was a missed opportunity. I just drifted through it. I wish people would understand how precious everything is now, in the moment—if I only knew then what I know now.*

Jemma's message sends out an alert. As the 15th century Sufi poet, Kabir put it, "Hiding in this cage of visible matter is the invisible life-bird. Pay attention to her, she is singing your song."

We miss opportunities at a global level as well. All around the world there are too many examples to count, but one that hits close to home for me is the situation in the Middle East. Palestine and Israel continue to miss opportunities for lasting peace. As Abba Eban put it, "the Palestinians never miss an opportunity to miss an opportunity."

The fall of the moderate Palestinian Prime Minister Mahmoud Abbas—destroyed by Yasser Arafat—represents such a missed opportunity on behalf of the Palestinians. Abbas was considered one of the leading Palestinian figures devoted to the search for a peaceful solution to the Palestinian-Israeli conflict. It was widely known that Abbas wanted to end the terror and collaborate with the United States to establish Palestine as an independent state. However, Arafat wanted to build a Palestinian state on the ruins of Israel. Continually undermined by Arafat from the beginning, Abbas, after a mere four months in office, was replaced by Ahmed Korei, whom many viewed as a "puppet" prime minister, whose strings were being pulled by Arafat.

For 56 years, every time the Palestinians were offered the possibility of a peaceful state alongside Israel, they chose to reject the offer and embark down a path of violence instead. In 1993 the Oslo accord was signed, bringing Arafat and the Palestine Liberation Organization (PLO) back to Palestine for what was supposed to be a historic reconciliation with Israel. However, even though Arafat had been offered 90% of what he wanted, rather than making peace and establishing new Palestinian institutions, he used the next decade to turn the Palestinian territories into armed camps in a renewed war against Israel.

Then the universe provided another chance to make peace. In 2004, Yasser Arafat was the president of the Palestine authority. At that time, the Rav knew the man that happened to be the chiropractor of the then Israeli Prime Minister, Ariel Sharon. Coincidentally we knew another man who was connected to Yasser Arafat. Both people independently approached my father, the Rav and asked if he would like to connect with these leaders to give them spiritual guidance and advice. After having a conversation with each man and building a rapport with them, my father saw the opportunity to try to bridge their differences, to perhaps really end this conflict.

In the end, even with my father's help, the discussions broke down and nothing was resolved. Six months later Arafat passed away, and Sharon had a massive stroke not too long afterwards. Who knows if this meeting was the reason they both came to this world, and who knows how many times their souls had brought them to a moment in which they could bring an end to a centuries-long conflict. But this opportunity for peace was lost, once more.

Missed opportunities are a huge source of pain for me. But jumping onto every opportunity that comes my way has taught me the importance of focus and planning. I have finally begun to understand why Ernest

Hemingway said, "Don't confuse movement with action." Given all that I have received and the lineage that I was born into, I find myself fretting that despite what I have been able to create and share with the world, I haven't done nearly as much as I could have. My challenge is to let some things go in order to follow through on my bigger goals. Now I am taking on the responsibility for choosing in every moment what is *really* a missed opportunity and what is just a distraction. I don't want to wake up at the age of 60 and feel that I had missed an opportunity to fulfill my potential because I was distracted. It's a bit like this story of the King and the Riddle Solver.

## The Symphony of Distraction

There once was a king who had a problem. He had a riddle that he needed to solve. So he made a declaration that he would grant anyone who solved the riddle access to the king's treasury for one hour, during which time they could take whatever they wanted. The next day, thousands of people lined up to solve the problem. And after many attempts, one man finally came up with the answer.

The king was pleased that now he knew the answer to the riddle. However, he began to regret that he had offered such a generous prize. So the king devised a plan. All night long, he and his advisors tirelessly researched the winner's life to see if they could figure out a way to distract him from paying attention to the king's treasure. By dawn, the king had his answer.

The man who had solved the riddle passionately loved classical music. So just before the allotted hour was set to begin, the king gathered together a spectacular symphony orchestra just outside the treasury room entrance. The riddle solver entered the treasury room and looked around. As soon as he was about to choose one of the crown jewels, the orchestra began to play. He stopped to take in the music, but after a while he caught himself. "Focus," he told himself, "I need to pay attention to the treasure."

Meanwhile, 15 minutes had passed. The man discovered a gold statue covered with jewels, and the symphony started again. This time a violin soloist played a melody that was simply exquisite. The man could not help himself, so he sat down to listen to the music in wonderment. Another 20 minutes went by. And then, before he could gather his resolve, a new piece began that continued for yet *another* 20 minutes.

Realizing that he only had five minutes of his allotted time remaining, the riddle solver decided to take a new approach. "What's the single most precious item here in the king's treasure house?" he asked himself. And then he saw an enormous diamond, its exquisitely cut facets gleaming. He rushed towards the glass case and was reaching for the diamond when he heard the most haunting melody, so beautiful that it made him weep. He was unable to move. The king had arranged to play this piece of music as the grand finale of distractions. Just as the music stopped and the man was about to grab the diamond, the king stopped him and said, "I'm sorry. Your time is up."

The riddle solver went home with absolutely nothing. He had an opportunity to take home vast riches from the king's personal treasury and he missed it. For a moment of pleasure, he passed up wealth for himself and his family.

* * *

By contrast, a man named Marc sent me an email about his missed opportunity. When I read it, it reminded me that for some, the opportunity is just to stay the course. See if his story has the same effect on you.

*Marc's Story*

*A few years ago, not long after being released from two years in prison, I was studying for a college degree in music. At the time all I wanted to do with my life was build a career in music. One day some people involved in making a movie in England came to the college to see if any of the students were interested in auditioning for a part. They were looking specifically for unknown actors. A couple of friends from my class really wanted to go to the audition, but I was a musician, not an actor!*

*However, just to appease my friends I ended up going along with them, and to my surprise, after being interviewed on camera and photographed, I was selected for the next stage of the audition process. I went along, and again I was selected for the next stage of the process. I ended up in a select group of 20 people out of the 1500 who originally auditioned! There were 10 or 15 parts to fill, and I was convinced that I was going to be picked. I was so sure I was going to be chosen for a part in the movie that I dropped out of college. I even convinced my bank manager I was about to become a movie star and talked him into an extension on my overdraft!*

*It turned out that I didn't get the part. I had left college, had a big overdraft to pay off, and felt as though somebody up there was playing tricks on me, like I had been cheated or made fun of in some way.*

*My missed opportunity was not completing my college course. By believing blindly that I would get the part, I let my ego get the better of me—big time. I ended up slipping back into the life I had lived before I had gone to prison—the life of a drug addict, selling drugs to pay for my own addiction. Three years later I ended up back in prison. I served two and a half more years for dealing drugs.*

*I hope this story may be of some use to you. I found my path in the end—more accurately, it found me, but I always think that if I had stayed on at college, and not given up everything by listening to my ego, I could have avoided a whole lot of pain for myself and others.*

For Marc the pain that he felt the second time he went to prison might have been what he needed to find his path. Often we are afraid to truly look inside ourselves. We feel guilt or shame over unresolved issues, and because we cannot handle looking further, we need to go through tremendous pain to open our eyes. If we don't fully wake up we will never figure out how we created the chaos in our lives, and we will never be able to change. One way or another we have to decide that we need to change. We have to decide to face all parts of our life head on. We *must* take full responsibility for ourselves.

As I was writing this chapter, I received a message on Twitter from a young woman whose grandmother had been murdered. My heart went out to this woman for her loss, and as it did I realized that the key for her to move through her pain was taking responsibility, not for what

**THE POWER TO CHANGE EVERYTHING**
CHAPTER FIVE: IT'S YOUR DECISION...

147

happened, but for what it was doing inside her. She could shut down and stop living her life or she could choose to honor her grandmother's memory by devoting herself to helping other murder victims. By recognizing that she is responsible for her own experience of her grandmother's death, she has an opportunity to make a change in herself for the better.

At the end of the day, the key is for *each* of us to take ultimate responsibility for all of our reactions to all of our experiences—the good and the chaotic. The Baal Shem Tov explains that *everything* that shows up in our life is our responsibility. Whatever enters into our lives is something we have to fully own. This may be difficult to accept in certain situations. How is it our responsibility that terrorists destroyed the World Trade Center? How can we be responsible if we were born with a deformity, or suffered from a childhood trauma?

Even if an event in our lives doesn't make sense in the context of this life experience, we have to accept that it's a lesson we need to learn from. It may even be a lesson held over from a previous incarnation. Fully understanding and accepting responsibility is the only way to begin to find happiness, fulfillment, and our purpose on this journey.

## WHAT IS RESPONSIBILITY, *REALLY*?

Eyes wide open. That's responsibility. When we take something upon ourselves, we have to make sure we accept the complete package, good and bad. For example, you might get into a relationship with someone who you *think* is absolutely amazing. Months later, you start to notice some flaws. You woke up from your infatuation and saw the entire picture. In truth, all of those things were there when you started the relationship—you just chose not to see them.

If you choose not to see, then whatever pain or disappointment you experience as a result is *your* responsibility. We cannot just look through the lens of our desires. We have to step back early on so that we fully understand what we are getting involved in. We have to keep our eyes wide open to see the full picture. We have to communicate and ask questions to get all of the facts. We have to accept what is really there, not just see what we want to see. Furthermore, once we understand, we must commit to seeing it through *completely*. We need to ask ourselves, 'Now that I see the whole picture, am I really prepared to take it on?" And, if we cannot say that we are fully prepared to go in, then we should decide to *not go in at all.* This is *a lot* of work, but this is what it means to take responsibility.

For many people this work implies a feeling of burden, or duty. "Responsibility" is usually the word that is tossed around in a negative context—when one has "screwed up." But responsibility isn't about pointing fingers or feeling burdened. It is about the *freedom* that comes when you and I are fully engaged. It's about making a decision based on the whole picture, knowing that you are willing to face a situation and that it is taking you in the right direction, even if you will not be able to control all of the factors.

There was a time in the early years of The Kabbalah Centre when my parents, the Rav and Karen, were tested by their decision to offer Kabbalah to anyone who sought out this wisdom. For thousands of years it had been limited to a select few. But they held on to their commitment to continue the work of The Kabbalah Centre. They knew going in that it would not be easy, but when you go in with eyes wide open, you can handle anything.

In 1984, I was 12 years old. At that age you don't always know exactly what's happening, but I had a sense that there was something big going on at The Kabbalah Centre. My father was ill and my mother was clearly under a lot of stress. Years later I learned what had actually happened: 21 of the 22 teachers at The Kabbalah Centre all decided to leave at the same time. My father had to make a decision. "Do I keep on going? Do I continue to spread this knowledge?"

Then my father realized that his uncertainty was an illusion challenging his commitment and responsibility. He resolved that teaching Kabbalah was *his* responsibility. He didn't know what would happen as a result of his efforts. He just knew he had to continue.

In our lives we usually do the opposite of what my father and mother did. We go into situations with our eyes closed. We follow an idea mindlessly, blinded by our ego or our good intentions. Then, once we are *fully* in the situation, we finally open our eyes—only to see that we are in it way over our heads. The regrettable truth is that good intentions will never get us very far.

This fact is exemplified in the story about a young kabbalist who was walking to his teacher's house to study. That day a powerful wind came up that made it difficult for him to walk. So he prayed for the wind to stop. When he had arrived at his teacher's home he heard that a plague had come upon the city. He asked his teacher the cause of the plague. And the teacher replied, "It was you. You prayed for the wind to stop, but the job of that wind was to blow away the vermin

150

**THE POWER TO CHANGE EVERYTHING**
CHAPTER FIVE: IT'S YOUR DECISION...

that carry the plague." As good as your intentions are, you cannot be of service if you don't see the big picture.

## WORLD PATTERNS

We are currently facing the effects of good intentions planted many years ago. The United States has a pattern of playing the superhero that helps out the rest of the world. As noble as this may sound, it has consistently created problems. The very nations that we intend to help suffer even greater problems than those we came to fix, and also find themselves in conflict with us. Think Vietnam. Cambodia. Iran. Iraq. Afghanistan.

U.S. policies in the 1970s contributed to the rise of the brutal Khmer Rouge who held power in Cambodia from 1975 to 1979. Washington agreed to support the *coup d'état* staged by the Khmer Rouge because we felt that the policies of the existing head of state, Norodom Sihanouk, benefited the communists in Vietnam, who were using Cambodian territory as a rear base and a supply line. However, an estimated 1.7 million Cambodians died from forced labor, starvation, medical neglect, and executions perpetrated by the Khmer Rouge regime.

At the beginning of the Iran-Iraq war in the early 1980s, the United States along with the Soviet Union, England, France, and Germany provided financing, intelligence, and military aid that allowed Saddam Hussein to turn Iraq into an aggressive military power. In 2003, the U.S. military, British forces, and smaller forces from Australia, Spain, Poland, and Denmark invaded Iraq "to disarm Iraq of weapons of mass destruction (WMD), to end Saddam Hussein's support for terrorism, and to free the Iraqi people." The result was

**THE POWER TO CHANGE EVERYTHING**
CHAPTER FIVE: IT'S YOUR DECISION...

151

tens of thousands of civilian deaths, widespread instability, and sectarian violence.

In an effort to diminish the Soviet Union's influence in the Middle East in the late '70s and early '80s, the Mujahedeen in Afghanistan were significantly financed and armed by the U.S. Central Intelligence Agency (CIA). U.S. support for the Mujahedeen evolved into an official U.S. foreign policy and, at one time, the Mujahedeen were praised by the U.S. as "freedom fighters." Ultimately, the Mujahedeen won a great victory when the Soviet Union pulled troops out of Afghanistan in 1989. And the U.S just walked away from the situation. Presently, one of the largest groups creating problems for the United States stems from the Mujahedeen "freedom fighters." They are known today as the Taliban.

Clearly we are not the only country that suffers from the good-intention syndrome; this is a world-wide issue. Venezuela has a cycle of forceful exchanges of power in the name of "the people." In fact, I was there during one such coup. My family was in town for an event at a Caracas hotel, and the day before the event I woke up to the sound of artillery shells and missiles. Looking out the window, we saw rebel soldiers shooting at our hotel, a place many foreigners frequented. Following instructions, my brother and I hid underneath our beds until we were called down to the basement. The hotel owner spoke to the authorities and promised that everything would be back to normal by the morning, which it was.

This incident was poignant for me, however, because I remember that during Hugo Chavez's brief moment of power, he took over the media and TV channels broadcast his speech to the nation. Standing with his machine gun next to him, the plan he outlined for the country

152

**THE POWER TO CHANGE EVERYTHING**
CHAPTER FIVE: IT'S YOUR DECISION...

sounded believable. He seemed to have genuinely good intentions to make Venezuela a "people's" country.

However, once the coup was put down, Carlos Perez, the president, made no changes to accommodate the forces behind the uprising. What's more, once Hugo Chavez himself was finally successful in taking over the country, he also failed to make the changes he had once promised. Having seen the fervor of Chavez's convictions first-hand, I don't doubt that he had good intentions.

When we walk into a situation without full awareness of what dynamics are really at play and we are not prepared to go the distance, this is not responsibility; this is the superhero syndrome at work. But superheroes only exist in comic books and movies. People or countries that have red capes in the closet usually create much more damage and drama than the problems they came to solve.

## THE MOMENT WILL *NOT* LAST FOREVER

When we look at things with eyes wide open, we no longer desire the lives of others. Instead, we appreciate the unique opportunities our challenges give us to achieve our destiny and overcome our limiting beliefs. So rather than look at someone else's relationship, look at the reason you may not be in one. You may be afraid of getting hurt; if so, the emptiness you feel from being alone can lead you to realize that real relationships are not perfect, they are a sticky mess. Sure, if you love you will get hurt, but the gift you will receive in return is an experience of unconditional sharing love, instead of insecure needy love. And the next thing you know, your soul mate will be at your door. Everything that comes to us is an opportunity for us to rise to our greatness.

## Switching Lives

There is a story about a king who ruled over a land where all of the people were dissatisfied with their lives. After listening to the grumblings of the people for a long time, he devised a brilliant plan. The people were instructed to each write down a list of everything that they "had" in life—money, health, a family, a big farm, a beautiful wife, etc. Then, on the other side of the paper, they were asked to write down everything that they lacked.

Everyone was then told to bring his or her pieces of paper to the center of town, where the king told his people that they could exchange cards with anyone they chose. However, they couldn't just take one side of the card; they had to take the entire package.

Excited, everyone ran to the center of town, eager to swap cards with the wealthiest man in the kingdom, but when they saw the back of his paper they realized that his marriage was loveless, his son was in jail, he hadn't spoken to his daughter in years, and he had five mistresses nagging him for his money: in short, he had no real love in his life; all people wanted was his wealth. Suddenly, no one wanted to trade with him.

Several other people approached the most powerful person in town. His authority was obvious—he influenced the town's policies, which shaped the lives of many people. However, when they discovered that he was sick and that despite all his influence he had not been able to find a cure, no one decided to take his sheet of paper either.

This process continued all day long. By the end of the day, everyone went home exhausted. After fully examining all of the other options in the town, each person had decided to keep the life they already had!

Until we open our eyes and see ourselves fully—good and bad—we might think that someone else is somehow better off. The first step to taking responsibility is to accept ourselves and our lives fully as they are; this is where our soul has placed us. Then we can see that everything is part of a *perfect* plan, and that the life we have is exactly the life we need.

## SATURN

Saturn's placement on our astrological chart indicates the area where we are most challenged. Looking at the location of Saturn during the time of our birth can help us recognize our blind spot—that place inside us where our fear keeps us from seizing the big opportunities, taking true responsibility, and accepting our purpose in this world. Known as the teacher, Saturn conveys the lessons of life that we are here to learn—however slowly. It has been suggested that the name Saturn comes from the Latin word *sator*, meaning to sow. Thus, the voice of Saturn often tells us what we have sowed and, therefore, what we deserve to reap. If we can own and recognize this part of ourselves, we can become better equipped to live according to our full potential. Those who fail to express the proactive nature of Saturn may find themselves in a reactive state—seeking security, hoping that an authority, partner, parent, or government will take care of things for them.

Use the following charts to determine where Saturn was at on the day you were born. Then review the information provided in the next several pages. This offers you an awareness of yourself that enables you to proactively work towards the changes you came into this world to make so you can take full responsibility for the life you came to lead.

## Where is your Saturn?

(1900 – 2050)

| | |
|---|---|
| January 1, 1900 – January 21, 1900 | Saturn in Sagittarius |
| January 22, 1900 – July 18, 1900 | Saturn in Capricorn |
| July 19, 1900 – October 17, 1900 | Saturn in Sagittarius |
| October 18, 1900 – January 20, 1903 | Saturn in Capricorn |
| January 21, 1903 – April 14, 1905 | Saturn in Aquarius |
| April 15, 1905 – August 17, 1905 | Saturn in Pisces |
| August 18, 1905 – January 9, 1906 | Saturn in Aquarius |
| January 10, 1906 – March 20, 1908 | Saturn in Pisces |
| March 21, 1908 – May 18, 1910 | Saturn in Aries |

| | |
|---|---|
| May 19, 1910 – December 15, 1910 | Saturn in Taurus |
| December 16, 1910 – January 20, 1911 | Saturn in Aries |
| January 21, 1911 – July 8, 1912 | Saturn in Taurus |
| July 9, 1912 – November 30, 1912 | Saturn in Gemini |
| December 1, 1912 – March 27, 1913 | Saturn in Taurus |
| March 28, 1913 – August 24, 1914 | Saturn in Gemini |
| August 25, 1914 – December 7, 1914 | Saturn in Cancer |
| December 8, 1914 – May 13, 1915 | Saturn in Gemini |
| May 14, 1915 – October 19, 1916 | Saturn in Cancer |
| October 20, 1916 – December 7, 1916 | Saturn in Leo |
| December 8, 1916 – June 25, 1917 | Saturn in Cancer |
| June 26, 1917 – August 13, 1919 | Saturn in Leo |
| August 14, 1919 – October 8, 1921 | Saturn in Virgo |

156

**THE POWER TO CHANGE EVERYTHING**
CHAPTER FIVE: IT'S YOUR DECISION...

| | |
|---|---|
| October 9, 1921 – December 21, 1923 | Saturn in Libra |
| December 22, 1923 – April 6, 1924 | Saturn in Scorpio |
| April 7, 1924 – September 14, 1924 | Saturn in Libra |
| September 15, 1924 – December 2, 1926 | Saturn in Scorpio |
| December 3, 1926 – March 16, 1929 | Saturn in Sagittarius |
| March 17, 1929 – May 5, 1929 | Saturn in Capricorn |
| May 6, 1929 – November 30, 1929 | Saturn in Sagittarius |
| December 1, 1929 – February 24, 1932 | Saturn in Capricorn |

| | |
|---|---|
| February 25, 1932 – August 13, 1932 | Saturn in Aquarius |
| August 14, 1932 – November 20, 1932 | Saturn in Capricorn |
| November 21, 1932 – February 15, 1935 | Saturn in Aquarius |
| February 16, 1935 – April 25, 1937 | Saturn in Pisces |
| April 26, 1937 – October 18, 1937 | Saturn in Aries |
| October 19, 1937 – January 14, 1938 | Saturn in Pisces |
| January 15, 1938 – July 7, 1939 | Saturn in Aries |
| July 8, 1939 – September 22, 1939 | Saturn in Taurus |
| September 23, 1939 – March 20, 1940 | Saturn in Aries |

| | |
|---|---|
| March 21, 1940 – May 8, 1942 | Saturn in Taurus |
| May 9, 1942 – June 21, 1944 | Saturn in Gemini |
| June 22, 1944 – August 2, 1946 | Saturn in Cancer |
| August 3, 1946 – September 18, 1948 | Saturn in Leo |
| September 19, 1948 – April 3, 1949 | Saturn in Virgo |
| April 4, 1949 – May 29, 1949 | Saturn in Leo |
| May 30, 1949 – November 20, 1950 | Saturn in Virgo |
| November 21, 1950 – March 7, 1951 | Saturn in Libra |
| March 8, 1951 – August 13, 1951 | Saturn in Virgo |

**THE POWER TO CHANGE EVERYTHING**
CHAPTER FIVE: IT'S YOUR DECISION...

157

| | |
|---|---|
| August 14, 1951 – October 23, 1953 | Saturn in Libra |
| October 24, 1953 – January 13, 1956 | Saturn in Scorpio |
| January 14, 1956 – May 15, 1956 | Saturn in Sagittarius |
| May 16, 1956 – October 11, 1956 | Saturn in Scorpio |
| October 12, 1956 – January 5, 1959 | Saturn in Sagittarius |
| January 6, 1959 – January 3, 1962 | Saturn in Capricorn |

| | |
|---|---|
| January 4, 1962 – March 24, 1962 | Saturn in Aquarius |
| March 25, 1962 – September 17, 1964 | Saturn in Pisces |
| September 18, 1964 – December 17, 1964 | Saturn in Aquarius |
| December 18, 1964 – March 3, 1967 | Saturn in Pisces |
| March 4, 1967 – April 30, 1969 | Saturn in Aries |
| May 1, 1969 – June 18, 1971 | Saturn in Taurus |

| | |
|---|---|
| June 19, 1971 – January 11, 1972 | Saturn in Gemini |
| January 12, 1972 – February 22, 1972 | Saturn in Taurus |
| February 23, 1972 – August 1, 1973 | Saturn in Gemini |
| August 2, 1973 – January 7, 1974 | Saturn in Cancer |
| January 8, 1974 – April 18, 1974 | Saturn in Gemini |
| April 19, 1974 – September 17, 1975 | Saturn in Cancer |
| September 18, 1975 – January 13, 1976 | Saturn in Leo |
| January 14, 1976 – June 5, 1976 | Saturn in Cancer |
| June 6, 1976 – November 17, 1977 | Saturn in Leo |
| November 18, 1977 – January 5, 1978 | Saturn in Virgo |
| January 6, 1978 – July 25, 1978 | Saturn in Leo |
| July 26, 1978 – September 21, 1980 | Saturn in Virgo |

158

**THE POWER TO CHANGE EVERYTHING**
CHAPTER FIVE: IT'S YOUR DECISION...

| | |
|---|---|
| September 22, 1980 – November 29, 1982 | Saturn in Libra |
| November 30, 1982 – May 6, 1983 | Saturn in Scorpio |
| May 7, 1983 – August 24, 1983 | Saturn in Libra |
| August 25, 1983 – November 17, 1985 | Saturn in Scorpio |
| November 18, 1985 – February 13, 1988 | Saturn in Sagittarius |
| February 14, 1988 – June 12, 1988 | Saturn in Capricorn |
| June 13, 1988 – November 13, 1988 | Saturn in Sagittarius |
| November 14, 1988 – February 6, 1991 | Saturn in Capricorn |

| | |
|---|---|
| February 7, 1991 – May 21, 1993 | Saturn in Aquarius |
| May 22, 1993 – June 30, 1993 | Saturn in Pisces |
| July 1, 1993 – January 28, 1994 | Saturn in Aquarius |
| January 29, 1994 – April 8, 1996 | Saturn in Pisces |
| April 9, 1996 – June 9, 1998 | Saturn in Aries |
| June 10, 1998 – August 11, 2000 | Saturn in Taurus |
| August 12, 2000 – October 17, 2000 | Saturn in Gemini |
| October 18, 2000 – April 21, 2001 | Saturn in Taurus |

| | |
|---|---|
| April 22, 2001 – June 4, 2003 | Saturn in Gemini |
| June 5, 2003 – July 16, 2005 | Saturn in Cancer |
| July 17, 2005 – September 2, 2007 | Saturn in Leo |
| September 3, 2007 – October 29, 2009 | Saturn in Virgo |
| October 30, 2009 – April 7, 2010 | Saturn in Libra |
| April 8, 2010 – July 21, 2010 | Saturn in Virgo |
| July 22, 2010 – October 6, 2012 | Saturn in Libra |

| | |
|---|---|
| October 7, 2012 – December 23, 2014 | Saturn in Scorpio |
| December 24, 2014 – June 15, 2015 | Saturn in Sagittarius |

**THE POWER TO CHANGE EVERYTHING**
CHAPTER FIVE: IT'S YOUR DECISION...

159

| | |
|---|---|
| June 16, 2015 – September 18, 2015 | Saturn in Scorpio |
| September 19, 2015 – December 19, 2017 | Saturn in Sagittarius |
| December 20, 2017 – March 22, 2020 | Saturn in Capricorn |
| March 23, 2020 – July 1, 2020 | Saturn in Aquarius |
| July 2, 2020 – December 18, 2020 | Saturn in Capricorn |

| | |
|---|---|
| December 19, 2020 – March 8, 2023 | Saturn in Aquarius |
| March 9, 2023 – May 25, 2025 | Saturn in Pisces |
| May 26, 2025 – September 2, 2025 | Saturn in Aries |
| September 3, 2025 – February 14, 2026 | Saturn in Pisces |
| February 15, 2026 – April 13, 2028 | Saturn in Aries |
| April 14, 2028 – June 1, 2030 | Saturn in Taurus |

| | |
|---|---|
| June 2, 2030 – July 14, 2032 | Saturn in Gemini |
| July 15, 2032 – August 28, 2034 | Saturn in Cancer |
| August 29, 2034 – February 15, 2035 | Saturn in Leo |
| February 16, 2035 – May 11, 2035 | Saturn in Cancer |
| May 12, 2035 – October 16, 2036 | Saturn in Leo |
| October 17, 2036 – February 11, 2037 | Saturn in Virgo |
| February 12, 2037 – July 7, 2037 | Saturn in Leo |
| July 8, 2037 – September 6, 2039 | Saturn in Virgo |
| September 7, 2039 – November 11, 2041 | Saturn in Libra |

| | |
|---|---|
| November 12, 2041 – June 21, 2042 | Saturn in Scorpio |
| June 22, 2042 – July 15, 2042 | Saturn in Libra |
| July 16, 2042 – February 22, 2044 | Saturn in Scorpio |
| February 23, 2044 - March 24, 2044 | Saturn in Sagittarius |
| March 25, 2044 - October 30, 2044 | Saturn in Scorpio |

| | |
|---|---|
| October 31, 2044 - January 23, 2047 | Saturn in Sagittarius |
| January 24, 2047 - July 10, 2047 | Saturn in Capricorn |
| July 11, 2047 - October 21, 2047 | Saturn in Sagittarius |
| October 22, 2047 - January 20, 2050 | Saturn in Capricorn |

| Saturn in Fire | Need to find creative efforts that define one's specialness. Deep residing fear of being ordinary and unimportant. | |
| --- | --- | --- |
| Saturn in Aries | *Proactive:*<br>• Need to feel powerful.<br>• Need to exert influence over the environment.<br>• Sense of security within oneself.<br>• Ability to express personal boundaries and limits.<br>• Able to live with life on life's terms. | *Reactive:*<br>• Lack of personal power.<br>• Fear of being controlled by others.<br>• Destructive competition.<br>• Feels pressured and bullied by others.<br>• Repression of inner desires.<br>• Resentments towards life. |
| Saturn in Leo | *Proactive:*<br>• Need to feel recognized.<br>• Need to feel appreciated.<br>• Strong sense of self and comfortable with his/her place in the world.<br>• Secure within one's own skin and with others.<br>• Comfortable being alone.<br>• Able to exist within a group and allow others to express their own uniqueness. | *Reactive:*<br>• Deep fear of being invisible.<br>• Overwhelming feelings of being unappreciated.<br>• Deep fear of being unimportant if he/she is not the center of attention.<br>• Unconscious dependence of others.<br>• Deep need for attention.<br>• Need to be the star of the show. |
| Saturn in Sagittarius | *Proactive:*<br>• Need to develop spiritual views to give purpose to life.<br>• Sense of having a connection to the Light and transforming that energy into inspiration.<br>• Understanding their purpose in life. | *Reactive:*<br>• Dogma and over-rigid structures that prevent meaningful spiritual growth.<br>• Fear of meaninglessness and feeling uninspired.<br>• Overbearing sense of self-importance. |

162

**THE POWER TO CHANGE EVERYTHING**
CHAPTER FIVE: IT'S YOUR DECISION...

| Saturn in Earth | Need to find security through the physical world in order to find a sense of self and inner security. | |
|---|---|---|
| Saturn in Taurus | *Proactive:*<br>• Need for familial and domestic security.<br>• Need to understand the natural cycles of growth and life.<br>• Ability to adapt to others and their needs.<br>• Able to accept help from others.<br>• Understands that in order to grow and develop we must move from level to level. | *Reactive:*<br>• Fear of the unpredictable.<br>• Fear of change.<br>• Stubbornness.<br>• Overly self-sufficient.<br>• Inability to change and evolve. |
| Saturn in Virgo | *Proactive:*<br>• Need to control the external world.<br>• Preoccupation with physical health.<br>• Deep understanding of the patterns of life. | *Reactive:*<br>• Fear of disorder and chaos.<br>• Hypochondria.<br>• Overcritical and obsessive thinking. |
| Saturn in Capricorn | *Proactive:*<br>• Need for order and tradition.<br>• Understanding that human nature needs to expand and grow in order to evolve.<br>• Understands that everyone has a need to be individual and express life in different and unique ways.<br>• Need for social standing. | *Reactive:*<br>• Fear of not belonging to a social group or tribe.<br>• Fear of chaotic aspects of human nature.<br>• Rigid definitions of social and sexual roles.<br>• Fear of having no purpose in life. |

| Saturn in Air | Need to find security through the world of ideals and thoughts that define one's personal viewpoint. | |
|---|---|---|
| Saturn in Gemini | *Proactive:*<br>• Need for knowledge and understanding.<br>• Understanding that truth is often subjective and in the eye of the beholder.<br>• Deep understanding that life is more than what meets the eye.<br>• Need to understand that others may have equally viable ideas and concepts.<br>• Desire to share with others to expand their own awareness. | *Reactive:*<br>• Fear of living in the unknown.<br>• Need for absolute or "the one" truth.<br>• Fear of being overwhelmed by the irrational.<br>• Rigidity of thinking.<br>• Desire to receive for the self alone. |
| Saturn in Libra | *Proactive:*<br>• Need to establish differences between right and wrong.<br>• Sharing with the right motivations.<br>• Clear defined ideals.<br>• Ability to express oneself without worrying about social position.<br>• Allows things to happen in their own time and season. | *Reactive:*<br>• Inability to make decisions and choices.<br>• Fear of being selfish or self centered.<br>• Inability to forge or articulate opinions.<br>• Politically correct.<br>• Perfectionist. |
| Saturn in Aquarius | *Proactive:*<br>• Need to preserve group values and ideals.<br>• Understanding that life provides us with opportunities to express our individual ideals and merits.<br>• Allows others to define their own "morality."<br>• Understanding that individual needs must be met in order to provide the group more vitality and growth. | *Reactive:*<br>• Inability to listen to others' ideals and accept the individual ideals of other people.<br>• Fear of being different and unique.<br>• Rigid moral standards.<br>• Over-identification with groups and social allegiances. |

164

**THE POWER TO CHANGE EVERYTHING**
CHAPTER FIVE: IT'S YOUR DECISION...

| Saturn in Water | Need to find personal security through relationships that define one's personal worth and self-esteem. | |
| --- | --- | --- |
| Saturn in Cancer | *Proactive:*<br>• A developed sense of self-love.<br>• Ability to stand on one's own two feet.<br>• Developed assertiveness.<br>• Comfortable being alone.<br>• Ability to develop one's own inner happiness. | *Reactive:*<br>• Needs guarantee of receiving love from others unconditionally.<br>• Fear of abandonment.<br>• Passivity and helplessness.<br>• Fear of rejection.<br>• Depression.<br>• Codependency. |
| Saturn in Scorpio | *Proactive:*<br>• Devout loyalty.<br>• Trusting the humanness of others.<br>• Comfortable with one's own accomplishments.<br>• Understands true love on a deep and profound level. | *Reactive:*<br>• Tendency towards deep suspicion of others.<br>• Fear of betrayal.<br>• Pride.<br>• Possessiveness.<br>• Emotional dominance over others. |
| Saturn in Pisces | *Proactive:*<br>• Need to feel emotionally connected to others.<br>• Self sacrifice.<br>• Ability to create healthy boundaries with others.<br>• Ability to develop a deep spiritual path and a need to connect to the Divine.<br>• Service to others. | *Reactive:*<br>• Fear of isolation.<br>• Fear of alienation.<br>• Giving to others in order to hold them emotionally close.<br>• Feelings of being victimized.<br>• Addictions.<br>• Dependency on others. |

# A WORK IN PROGRESS

I hope you've taken away some useful ideas from these pages. In them I've shared with you the issues that keep me awake at night and the issues that give me soaring hope. Together we've explored my belief that enacting real change is not the job of politics or religion; it's down to us, to each one of us individually, to change ourselves—and thereby our world.

How do we do it? The answer lies in recognizing the single biggest obstacle that trips us: ego. And once we see this, we need to recognize the transformative power of living the insight each and every day, of making this particular choice because it diminishes ego and that particular choice because it supports selfless sharing, for these are two sides of the same precious coin.

These choices we make are usually not earthshaking, they're the hundreds of little decisions we make every day: to act or not to act; to give or to hold back. However minor they may seem, each one of these crossroads gives us an opportunity that extends way beyond the given moment, and perhaps even beyond this lifetime. Thankfully, the Creator gave us free will so we could make these choices, and in this gift lies both our challenge and our salvation.

In a way it all boils down to this: There are two ways of being in this world. The primitive approach is to live by short-term solutions, suffer from emptiness, and feel only moments of real happiness, fearful of what tomorrow will bring for you and the world. Hopefully after reading this book, this is not the option you'll choose.

The other choice is to accept and appreciate everything and everyone in our path, knowing that they have been placed in this world to help us achieve perfection. When we adopt this approach, obstacles no longer bother us in the same way. Now we understand that the longing we experience is not for material possessions and external status. Instead, that longing is the soul's desire to reach the perfection for which we and the world were created.

Most life-map or personal goal coaching systems work to take us away from where we are now to where we want to be. Yet there's a fundamental flaw in this approach. An example of a more successful method is in any creative field where ideas manifest into reality—such as in the music industry, the book publishing industry, and the movie industry. These industries begin by setting the date for release and then work backwards to establish benchmarks and short-term goals. We need to work in this same way to achieve our life plan. We need to work backward from our perfected self.

By envisioning the destination, we can locate the best steps to take us there. I am not talking merely about living in the present because one interpretation of living in the present is simply to react to what life throws our way. I am talking about a focus on the future so you can be proactive in the present—realizing that every day contains opportunities for us to take actions that will bring ourselves—and the world—closer to perfection.

When God first had a vision of this world it was perfect, and this vision formed the basis of God's plan for Creation. The following exercise will help you discover your perfected self and life path (it is a given that everyone will have a different vision and plan). There is no one way to do this; you need to do it in a way that works for you. But don't skip over it. You are not finished with this book until you take the time to complete this exercise. This is the moment. Seize your opportunity!

Take some time to really think about your perfected self. This is not easy, so don't rush it. Pull out a journal or notebook, and write down your vision in as much detail as possible. What would your perfect "me" look like in all the areas of your life: your relationships—loves, friendships, business connections; your finances and livelihood—how would you live, what would you do, how much would you earn? What about your physical well-being? What would your body look like, feel like? What would your mind, your emotions, and your spiritual life be like? Connect to the whole picture of your perfection without limitations or fears. Perfection is unlimited. Your vision of your perfected self should be as unlimited as the possibilities, so really stretch your mind.

Once you have completed this part of the.exercise, write down where you are in your life right now, in just as much detail as possible. What is working in your life and why? What is not working? The key here is to be honest. When you are truthful, the universe will be most able to help you.

There is no limit to what we can accomplish, however you also have to be realistic: if you want to be an opera singer and simply do not have the voice, chances are that you are not meant to be an opera singer. Our souls have given us everything we need to reach our individual perfection. Our gifts are perfectly matched to this purpose. Not telling yourself the truth will only delay the process. Remember, whatever you say stays between you and God.

Now that you have a destination and a sense of your present whereabouts, you can begin to map out your plan. A vision is just an idea until you make a commitment to integrate its pursuit into your everyday life. Create real and manageable goals. How will you proactively move towards these goals? What changes will you make in your daily life? On what timetable? Is yours a one-, three-, or five-year plan? What behaviors and belief systems will you choose to eliminate? What new practices will you incorporate? What will your life look like at the end of year one, year three, or year five?

People tend to underestimate the importance of the vision and overestimate the importance of the goals. Take care that your short-term goals are not too lofty. A year goes by quickly. And if you don't meet your goals, don't abandon ship. Remember that 95 percent of the work takes place at the beginning. Revisit your goals and remember, too, that your arrival at your perfect self is guaranteed. That is the promise of Creation. If you are not meeting your short-term goals, don't let yourself become depressed or angry. It simply means there is more work to do. Just know without a shadow of doubt that you cannot help but make decisions that will bring about global perfection, as well as your own perfection. This is your destiny.

In closing, I would like to leave you with Rav Ashlag's three simple concepts to live by in working towards our perfection.

1. **Don't lie to yourself.**

2. **Perfection comes with some sort of sacrifice.**

3. **Embrace the constant battle to overcome the ego.**

You are on your way to your perfected self. You are on your way to changing everything.

# MORE BY YEHUDA BERG

### *The Power of Kabbalah*

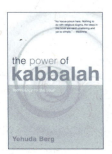

Imagine your life filled with unending joy, purpose, and contentment. Imagine your days infused with pure insight and energy. This is *The Power of Kabbalah*. It is the path from the momentary pleasure that most of us settle for, to the lasting fulfillment that is yours to claim. Your deepest desires are waiting to be realized. Find out how, in this basic introduction to the ancient wisdom of Kabbalah.

### *The Living Kabbalah System™: Level 1*

Take Your Life to the Next Level™ with this step-by-step, 23-day system for transforming your life and achieving lasting fulfillment.

Created by Yehuda Berg and based on his belief that Kabbalah should be lived, not merely studied, this revolutionary interactive system incorporates the latest learning strategies, addressing all three learning styles:

- Auditory (recorded audio sessions)

- Visual (workbook with written concepts and graphics)

- Tactile (written exercises, self-assessments, and physical tools)

The sturdy carrying case makes the system easy and convenient to use, in the car, at the gym, on a plane, wherever and whenever you choose. Learn from today's great Kabbalah leaders in an intimate, one-on-one learning atmosphere. You get practical, actionable tools and exercises to integrate the wisdom of Kabbalah into your daily life. In just 23 days you can learn to live with greater intensity, be more successful in business and relationships, and achieve your dreams. Why wait? Take your life to the next level starting today.

## Readers Take Action Program with Eco-Libris

Founded in 2007, Eco-Libris (www.ecolibris.net) is a green company that works with book readers, publishers, authors, bookstores and others in the book industry to make reading more sustainable.

More than 30 million trees are cut down annually for virgin paper used for the production of books sold in the U.S. alone. Eco-Libris aims to raise awareness to the environmental impacts of using paper for the production of books and provide people and businesses with an affordable and easy way to do something about it: plant one tree for every book they read, publish or sell.

We invite you to take action and balance out your books with Eco-Libris on their website—www.ecolibris.net/yehudaberg.asp. For every book you balance out, you will receive a sticker made of recycled paper saying "One tree planted for their book", which you can display on your book shelves. For every five trees planted on your behalf, one more tree will be planted on behalf of Kabbalah Publishing as an appreciation of their commitment to the environment.

To achieve these goals, Eco-Libris partnered with three highly respected US and UK registered non-profit organizations that work in collaboration with local communities in developing countries to plant these trees. These trees are planted in high ecological and sustainable standards in Latin America and Africa, where deforestation is a crucial problem. Planting trees in these places not only helps to fight climate change and conserve soil and water, but also benefits many local people, for whom these trees offer many benefits, such as improvement of crops and additional food and income, and an opportunity for a better future.

In loving memory and elevation of the soul of my beloved father

Fajwel Rajczyk

(Hebrew: Feivel ben Avrum Halevy)

May the Light of the Zohar and the Creator shine upon

my son Reuben

my husband Mitchell

my brother Eddy, his wife Julie,

and his children Adam, Ashley, Danny, and Jenna

May we all be blessed with love, wisdom, understanding, freedom,

gratitude, and meaningful lives

Judy Cayen